新开端英语专业基础课系列教材

Extensive Reading
阅读拓展
Yuedu Tuozhan

3
学生用书
（第2版）

总主编 戚 涛　胡 健
主　编 朱蕴轶
副主编 王 敏

北京师范大学出版社集团
BEIJING NORMAL UNIVERSITY PUBLISHING GROUP
安徽大学出版社

图书在版编目（CIP）数据

阅读拓展（3）学生用书 / 朱蕴轶主编. --2版. -- 合肥：安徽大学出版社，2024.8
ISBN 978-7-5664-2803-5

Ⅰ.①阅… Ⅱ.①朱… Ⅲ.①英语—阅读教学—高等学校—教材 Ⅳ.① H319.37

中国国家版本馆 CIP 数据核字（2024）第 023474 号

出版发行：	北京师范大学出版集团
	安 徽 大 学 出 版 社
	（安徽省合肥市肥西路3号 邮编230039）
	www.bnupg.com
	www.ahupress.com.cn
印　　刷：	安徽利民印务有限公司
经　　销：	全国新华书店
开　　本：	880 mm×1230 mm　1/16
印　　张：	12.75
字　　数：	408 千字
版　　次：	2024 年 8 月第 2 版
印　　次：	2024 年 8 月第 1 次印刷
定　　价：	45.00 元

ISBN 978-7-5664-2803-5

策划编辑：李　雪		装帧设计：李　雪　李　军	
责任编辑：李　雪		美术编辑：李　军	
责任校对：高婷婷		责任印制：陈　如　孟献辉	

版权所有　侵权必究

反盗版、侵权举报电话：0551-65106311
外埠邮购电话：0551-65107716
本书如有印装质量问题，请与印制管理部联系调换。
印制管理部电话：0551-65106311

前 言

在信息膨胀、知识爆炸的今天，面对数量庞大、纷繁芜杂的观点和信息，高效获取有价值的信息、辨识和评判各种观点，成了现代人的必备技能。因此，在高等英语教育中，提升学生的阅读能力，尤其是批判性阅读的能力成为了一项重要任务，这也对阅读教材的编写提出了更高的要求。作为英语专业的泛读教材，本教材在安徽省"十一五"规划教材《阅读拓展》（1~4册）的基础上进行修订。受时代因素所限，旧版教材存在文字相对陈旧、选材视野不宽、练习较为单调、缺乏思维训练等诸多缺憾。为应对国家培养复合型、创新型高素质英语人才的需求和AI时代提出的新挑战，本团队对旧版教材进行了大幅修改，其中第1册更新比例为70%，其余3册更新比例为100%。最突出的变化是：旧版教材局限在扩大词汇量及提高阅读能力；新版教材则着眼于阅读、批判性思维、跨文化交际、价值观等能力与素养的综合提升，尤其是第3、4册，突出了批判性阅读能力的训练。

教材第1、2册着重介绍英语阅读的常见技巧，旨在帮助学生在保证信息获取准确度的前提下，进一步提升阅读速度，从而提高阅读效率。第1、2册各8个单元，每单元有一个相对独立的主题，介绍一个主要的阅读技巧，包括快速获取主旨大意、通过上下文猜测词义、区分观点与事实等。

第1、2册每单元均分为Before Reading、While Reading、After Reading 3个部分。Before Reading部分起到课程导入的作用，形式丰富多样，有传统的课前讨论、词汇头脑风暴，也有新型的思维导图绘制及海报制作等。While Reading部分选材广泛，主题多样，涉及政治、经济、文化、环保、文学、社会等领域。所选文本长度与难度适中，一般为1000词左右，适合课堂教学及学生自学。文后配套练习的形式主

Extensive Reading 3

要包括阅读理解、判断正误、词汇配对、选词填空、读后讨论等，引导和帮助学生完成整个阅读过程。同时为了发挥"以读促写"的作用，部分单元还设计了相关的写作练习。After Reading 部分是学生深度思考和扩展知识的一个重要环节。此部分有扩展练习 Extension Exercise 和素养提升 Value Cultivation 等方面内容。Value Cultivation 每单元有不同主题，是传扬中国传统美德或其他类型价值正能量的课程思政内容，贴近学生的生活和学习，以"润物细无声"的方式帮助学生树立正确的人生观和世界观。此外，第1、2册还有机融入了跨文化交际意识和能力的培养。对于阅读文本中出现的文化差异、文化常识等内容均配有相应的注释或介绍，目的是在英语学习的基础阶段培养学生对跨文化交际的敏感性及对待文化差异的正确态度。

教材第3、4册在阅读技能提升的基础上，将批判性思维和课程思政融入英语阅读训练中，旨在帮助学生理解、分析和评判各种观点背后隐藏的逻辑，在此基础上学会选择与社会主义核心价值观相协调的价值立场。第3、4册各8个单元，内容涵盖批判性阅读的概念和相关理论、常用批判性阅读策略、基本论证类型和论证逻辑结构、逻辑推理知识以及常见逻辑谬误等，以阅读能力的提高为"驱动力"，旨在全面提升学生的批判性思维能力和英语综合应用能力，使学生能够对作者的观点、态度、假设、论证等进行分析、整合和评判，能够独立思考、提出问题、分析问题、解决问题。

第3、4册每个单元围绕1个批判性阅读相关概念或者策略展开，并提供2篇阅读材料。文章选自英语国家近年来出版的图书与网络材料，或节选自经典英文作品，其中很大一部分来自 BBC, *The Economist*, www.nytimes.com, *Time*, *The Washington Post*, *Scientific American* 等知名报刊杂志与网站，题材涉及教育、科技、语言、历史、艺术、文学、文化等诸多领域。文章均经过精挑细选，长度适中，难度相宜，少数地方做了必要的改写与删减。多数单元的理论介绍之后辅以巩固练习。每单元的两篇课文前均有 Preparatory Work 和课文导入，帮助学生调动图式背景，激发阅读兴趣，了解课文重点。文章后的 Notes 帮助学生了解文章背景和相关知识；文章后的练习根据 Bloom 教育目标分类表的 6 个层级，分为 Remembering and Understanding、Reasoning and Analyzing 和 Reflecting and Creating 3 个部分，并着重融入本单元的批判性阅读策略和技巧。3 个部分的练习内容丰富、形式活泼，主要有填空题、是非判断题、选择题、简答题、讨论题、画图题、短文写作等。单元最后有 3 个总结部分。Self-reflection 部分帮助学生反思本单元重难点的掌握情况。Value Cultivation 部分是课程思政内容，结合本单元话题，力求培养学生求真务实、开拓进取的治学态度和科学观，使学生具有高尚的道德情操、健全的人格、较高的人文素养；认同和坚持优秀的中华传统文化，具备辨别东西方文化中不同价值观的基本素质；具有党和国家意识以及社会主义核心价值观，既具有宽广的国际视野又具有爱国主义情怀。Further Reading 部分是拓展阅读推荐，供学生课后进一步拓展相关话题的阅读量和知识面。

本套教材适合作为英语专业的教材，供第 1 至第 4 学期的教学使用，每学期 1 册。

本次修订工作由安徽大学戚涛教授、胡健教授主持，全面负责教材的资料筛选、阅读技巧的编排、练习题型和题量的设定，以及定稿前的主审工作。教材编写具体分工如下：第 1 册张丽红老师编写第 1、5、7、8 单元，朱玲麟老师编写第 2、3、4、6 单元；第 2 册张丽红老师编写第 2、4、7、8 单元，朱玲麟老师编写第 1、3、5、6 单元；第 3 册朱蕴轶老师编写第 1、2、3、8 单元，王敏老师编写第 4、5、6、7 单元；第 4 册朱蕴轶老师编写第 1、4、5、8 单元，王敏老师编写第 2、3、6、7 单元。中国科技大学外籍教师 Murray Wayne Sherk 负责后期语言审校工作。

虽然编写工作历时 2 年，编者也皆为从教多年的高校教师，但我们仍恐教材存在疏漏不妥之处，欢迎同行专家不吝赐教！

编 者

2024 年 7 月

★ CONTENTS ★

Unit 1 Critical Reading: A General Introduction 1
   Mastering Critical Reading 2
   Text A Inside the Infodemic: Coronavirus in the Age of Wellness 6
   Text B How Can We Learn to Reject Fake News in the Digital World? 15
   Summary 25

Unit 2 Getting Started 27
   Mastering Critical Reading 28
   Text A How to Mark a Book 31
   Text B How Come the Quantum 42
   Summary 52

Unit 3 Learning to Ask Questions 55
   Mastering Critical Reading 56
   Text A The Man Who Asked Questions (Excerpt) 60
   Text B The Symposium (Excerpt) 69
   Summary 78

Unit 4 Understanding Arguments: The Basics 81
   Mastering Critical Reading 82
   Text A Your Brain Lies to You 85
   Text B Why Doubt Is Essential to Science 91
   Summary 98

Extensive Reading 3

Unit 5 Key Elements of Arguments: Definition 101
Mastering Critical Reading 102
Text A Crossing the Aegean Is "Traumatic". Your Bad Hair Day Isn't 105
Text B Knowledge and Wisdom (Excerpt) 112
Summary 118

Unit 6 Key Elements of Arguments: Claim 121
Mastering Critical Reading 122
Text A Letter from Birmingham Jail (Excerpt) 125
Text B How Food Influencers Affect What We Eat 134
Summary 145

Unit 7 Key Elements of Arguments: Support 149
Mastering Critical Reading 150
Text A Are Women Really More Talkative Than Men? 153
Text B Who Does the Talking Here? 160
Summary 166

Unit 8 Key Elements of Arguments: Assumptions 169
Mastering Critical Reading 170
Text A The Higher Education Learning Crisis 173
Text B What Would Plato Say About ChatGPT? 183
Summary 193

Unit 1
Critical Reading: A General Introduction

Mastering Critical Reading

Like it or not, we are now living in a real "information explosion" age. Highly developed science and technology give us easy and varied access to a huge amount of information containing both true and false data. Therefore, the ability to distinguish, to think, and to reason, is essential in all walks of life.

In any context, it is important not to assume that everything we encounter in our reading is merely a straightforward presentation of facts. In every field of study, numerous perspectives exist, requiring us to understand not only what writers are saying, but how and why they are saying it. This understanding is crucial for evaluating the reliability and validity of the information and arguments presented. Consequently, engaging in critical reading becomes essential.

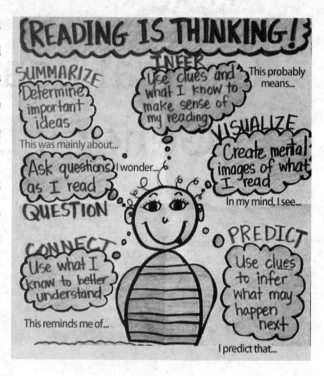

■ **What Is Critical Reading?**

According to Elizabeth Browning, "Critical reading is the process of analyzing and evaluating a text by carefully considering its content, structure, and context." To read critically is to assess how a text presents and supports its arguments. It is a skill that demands reflection and the ability to step back from the text to gain perspective. It involves not only understanding what an author is saying but analyzing and evaluating what and how the author is communicating, and forming our own opinions about them.

■ **Qualities for Critical Reading**

Critical reading does not just involve accumulating knowledge or superficial understanding. It is also a way to make sensible judgments and draw sound conclusions. Critical readers think clearly and rationally, and they make logical connections between ideas instead of blindly accepting whatever comes to them. They focus on facts and rational analysis and evaluation of the information at hand. To build this ability, we should equip ourselves with the following qualities to get prepared:

❖ Curiosity
❖ Honesty

Unit 1 Critical Reading: A General Introduction

- ❖ Open-mindedness
- ❖ Rationality
- ❖ Analytical thinking
- ❖ Being reflective

■ Thinking Critically About What You Read

Critical thinking enables us to monitor our comprehension while reading. While it is necessary to evaluate ideas during the reading process, it is important to avoid distorting the intended meaning of the text. We must refrain from imposing our own desired interpretation onto the text. Bloom's Taxonomy divides the way people learn into six levels, which can be used in teaching critical thinking.

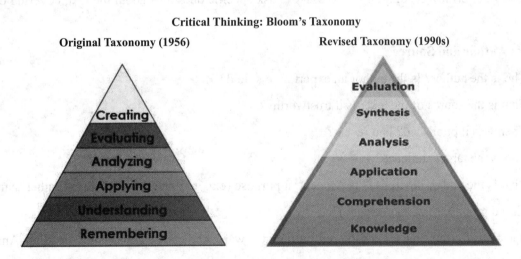

■ Incorporation of Critical Thinking in Reading

The levels of reading can be arranged as a hierarchy from literal reading at the bottom, to inferential reading in the middle, and finally to evaluative reading at the top. Each level has a purpose and incorporates different critical thinking strategies.

Extensive Reading 3

Reading Level	Thinking Level	Thinking
Evaluative	Creating	What would it be like if…? *create, develop, generate, produce, imagine*
Evaluative	Evaluating	Why do you think that…? *conclude, debate, justify, judge, assess*
Inferential	Analyzing	What other ways could…? *categorize, dissect, examine, compare, contrast*
Inferential	Applying	How would you solve…? *apply, demonstrate, implement, practice*
Literal	Understanding	What is the main idea of…? *describe, explain, paraphrase, retell*
Literal	Remembering	Who, What, When, Where…? *cite, define, find, list*

■ How to Read Critically

To engage in critical reading, it is necessary to ask specific questions about the text, covering three key areas:

First Area: Author and Source

1. Who is the author? Is the author an expert in this field?
2. What is the source of the text? Is it trustworthy?
3. When was it published? Is it recent?
4. Who is the target audience?
5. What is the author's purpose? Is it a neutral purpose (e.g., to explain or to inform) rather than a more biased purpose (e.g., to persuade)?

❖ Questions for this area are mostly quite straightforward, and can be asked before reading. Answers to these questions may help us decide whether the text is worth reading at all.

Second Area: Evidence and Reasoning

1. How strong is the evidence? Is the reasoning valid?
2. Does the author avoid making unsupported generalizations?
3. Is there a clear distinction between fact and the author's opinion?
4. Are there proper citations used? If so, are the sources cited considered reliable and up-to-date?
5. In the case of a research article, is the methodology valid (e.g., sample size, sampling method)? Are

the limitations explicitly stated? Do the results align with the stated objectives?

Look at the argument and examine its validity:

> **?**
>
> Traditional print journalism is dying. The proliferation of online and cable news sources makes it easy for readers to bypass newspapers and magazines.
> ✓ What is the generalization made in the argument?
> ✓ What is the evidence given in support of the generalization?
> ✓ Is the reasoning valid?

❖ Questions for this area pose a greater challenge compared to those of the first area, as they require careful reading of the text and thoughtful analysis of its meaning.

Third Area: Assumptions and Bias

1. What assumptions does the author make? Are they valid?
2. What is the author's stance on the topic? Is it clearly expressed?
3. Does the author present a balanced viewpoint, considering other perspectives?
4. Are the author's conclusions reasonable based on the evidence?
5. Is the author's language neutral, avoiding emotional language and bias?

Look at the argument and identify the assumption:

> **?**
>
> Traditional print journalism is dying. The proliferation of online and cable news sources makes it easy for readers to bypass newspapers and magazines.
> ✓ What is the hidden assumption in the argument?
> ✓ Are you willing to grant the author's assumptions?

❖ Questions for this area are the most challenging. They allow readers to delve deeper into the text and evaluate various elements.

Extensive Reading 3

Text A Inside the Infodemic: Coronavirus in the Age of Wellness

Preparatory Work

Illustration used for the 1st WHO Infodemiology Conference and the webinar on Infodemic Management of 23 September. Credit: WHO/Sam Bradd

Credit: Getty Images

Activity 1 Brainstorming

During the COVID-19 pandemic, we saw a huge volume of inaccurate and even harmful information proliferating over social media, leaving people confused, misled, and wrongly-advised. Brainstorm and list several examples of false information about COVID-19 you have come across on social media platforms. You may think about various types of false information: conspiracy theories, fake remedies, misleading statistics, inaccurate prevention methods, etc.

Unit 1 Critical Reading: A General Introduction

Types	False information
Conspiracy theories	
Fake remedies	
Misleading statistics	
Inaccurate prevention methods	
Others	

Credit: united-nations-COVID-19-response-zw3ExyW6x3Y-unsplash-e1592406874260.jpg

Activity 2 Facts, False Information, or Opinions

The following are statements about COVID-19. Decide whether they are facts, false information, or opinions.

( ) 1. Drinking bleach or other disinfectants can cure COVID-19.

( ) 2. The economic impact of COVID-19 is more damaging than the health consequences.

( ) 3. Common symptoms of COVID-19 include fever, cough, shortness of breath, fatigue, loss of taste or smell, and body aches.

( ) 4. The media has exaggerated the severity of COVID-19, causing unnecessary panic.

( ) 5. 5G networks spread COVID-19.

( ) 6. Vaccines have been developed and approved for COVID-19, providing protection against the virus.

( ) 7. Wearing masks in public places should be mandatory to prevent the transmission of COVID-19.

( ) 8. Only older people are at risk of contracting COVID-19.

( ) 9. Governments should implement strict lockdown measures to control the spread of COVID-19.

( ) 10. COVID-19 is a hoax created to control the population.

Extensive Reading 3

Reading the Text

> Fake news, propaganda, and conspiracy theories, ubiquitous in the era of social media, have spread since the beginning of the COVID-19 pandemic. These cause confusion and risk-taking behaviors that can harm health. They also lead to mistrust in health authorities and undermine the public health response. An infodemic can intensify or lengthen outbreaks when people are unsure about what they need to do to protect their health and the health of people around them.

Inside the Infodemic: Coronavirus in the Age of Wellness

As the disease spreads, so do quack "cures" such as garlic, bleach and silver solution, peddled on social media.

—*Sabrina Weiss[1]*

Garlic, magic pills, silver flakes. (Photo by, from left to right: Pixabay via Canva, Shutterstock, Marketplace Designers via Canva)

1 Online misinformation about the novel coronavirus disease, now called COVID-19, appears to be spreading faster than the virus itself. Certain claims made about the origins and transmission of the virus may be true, but many aren't, and these falsehoods are fuelling conspiracy theories that serve only to spread fear on a global scale. The World Health Organisation (WHO) has labelled the overabundance of information an "infodemic", arguing it "makes it hard for people to find trustworthy sources and reliable guidance when they need it".

2 Scientists need time to study the new disease and test potential vaccines and treatments, which permits quacks to fill the vacuum. People who feel scared, helpless and desperate easily fall into the trap of the alternative remedies that have been cropping up across the web. One example is a bogus message that has been doing the rounds on WhatsApp[2], suggesting a "senior doctor's" recipe for boiled garlic water can cure the disease. An extra dose of vitamin C is said to ward off the infection in the first place, just as it would in a

common cold. These home remedies promise inexpensive and effective protection.

3   Neither of these claims is true and there is currently no vaccine or cure available for the virus that has, at the time of writing, killed nearly 2,118 people and infected 74,576 since December. But that doesn't hold opportunists back from cashing in on fears over the virus by spreading false information and selling dubious health and wellness products online.

4   There may be no harm in drinking a bowl of freshly boiled garlic water or adding vitamin C supplements to your daily routine, but there is a risk that, for some, these remedies provide a false sense of security and undermine the efforts of health officials to curb the spread of the disease.

5   Other claims could do more harm than good: "Miracle Mineral Solutions", referred to as MMS, have been sold online as a cure-all for cancer, HIV, autism and now coronavirus. A common MMS liquid solution consists of 28 percent sodium chlorite in distilled water, essentially a potent bleaching agent that can cause severe vomiting, diarrhoea and acute liver failure.

Miracle Mineral Solution (MMS) is a product created by Jim Humble, an ex-Scientologist who now styles himself as "archbishop" of the Genesis II Church of Health & Healing

6   Everyone from self-proclaimed experts to anti-vaccination proponents to faith healers has something to say about the possible cures for coronavirus. Some may mean well and want to share any news in the face of an outbreak where the disease is novel and there are still many unknowns, while others are seeking the attention that will drive traffic to their own channels.

7   Most individuals are motivated to spread false information in order to monetise in one way or another, as Danny Rogers, co-founder of the London-based nonprofit Global Disinformation Index[3], points out. They are aggregating user attention to game the ad-tech system or profiting from selling advertising space and merchandise on their websites—in much the same way as Gwyneth Paltrow's[4] wellness and lifestyle company Goop does. Ultimately, the old advertising adage "money follows eyeballs" still applies in the age of online misinformation.

8   Sather doesn't sell MMS directly but does peddle dietary supplements starting from $32 (£24), and Rivera has written a number of "cure" and cookbooks. Others actually have quack cures on offer: in an online episode of his show on 12 February, the conservative televangelist Jim Bakker suggests his $125 (£96) "silver solution" can eliminate coronaviruses within 12 hours and boost the immune system.

Extensive Reading 3

Televangelist Jim Bakker claims his magic "silver solution" cures coronavirus

⁹ Tara Kirk Sell, a senior scholar at the Johns Hopkins Center for Health Security[5], says she understands why some people might be more receptive to inexpensive home remedies like garlic or vitamin C, as there is less tendency to trust in experts, authority, mainstream media and medicine when there aren't many answers available.

¹⁰ The Internet can also be an ally in the fight against infectious diseases. Since the COVID-19 epidemic unfolded, the WHO and scientists have been using social media to counter misinformation and to share messages about protective measures.

¹¹ "The real value of scientists talking about the disease on Twitter is that the scientific discoveries related to this outbreak are spread much more quickly and there's a lot more access for both other scientists and the public," says Sell.

¹² In a concerted effort with the WHO, social media firms are taking steps to remove false claims and promote accurate information. Twitter users in the UK who search for "coronavirus cure" are prompted to visit the Department of Health and Social Care website and a Facebook search surfaces primarily posts from government, health organisations and traditional media; the company is also working with independent fact-checkers to label inaccurate posts and delete dubious health advice.

¹³ Google—which in December was still running sponsored ads for MMS alongside its search results—rolled out an SOS alert service on 31 January, which sends users to a curated search results page with information and reports from the WHO and major news organisations.

¹⁴ "It shows interventions are possible and can work when the platforms are motivated to act," says Danny Rogers. Dealing with misinformation around public health emergencies may be easier than political campaigns because COVID-19 is not a voting or paying constituency. "Everyone can agree on a common enemy here," he says.

¹⁵ As for the proliferating quack cures for coronavirus, an analysis undertaken by monitoring firm Social360 for this article showed some UK media have been sharing (and in some cases debunking) stories about the touted bleach, garlic and silver cures on Twitter—with limited traction—which may be due to the fact that the virus hasn't spread as widely in the UK yet. However, such social media searches exclude private

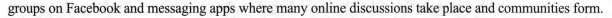

Unit 1 Critical Reading: A General Introduction

groups on Facebook and messaging apps where many online discussions take place and communities form.

16 Twitter, Facebook and Google's filters and algorithms may be a good starting point in tackling misinformation about coronavirus and allow people to easily find relevant and authoritative updates. However, penetrating the social media echo chambers fuelled by distrust in experts and news outlets will be the real challenge.

(Source: *New Statesman,* Feburary 20, 2020.)

Notes

1. **Sabrina Weiss** is a London-based science journalist and author.
2. **WhatsApp** is a popular instant messaging application owned by Meta. It allows users to send text messages, make voice and video calls, share photos, videos, documents, location, and other media files with their contacts. WhatsApp uses end-to-end encryption, which means that the messages and calls are secured and can only be accessed by the intended recipients.
3. **The Global Disinformation Index** (GDI) is an independent, and non-profit organization that aims to combat disinformation and promote trusted information sources in order to create a more informed and resilient society. The organization was founded in 2017 and is based in London.
4. **Gwyneth Paltrow** is an American actress, businesswoman, and author. Born in 1972, she made her acting debut in the early 1990s and gained widespread recognition for her performances in films such as *Emma, Shakespeare in Love,* and *Iron Man.* Paltrow has received numerous awards and accolades throughout her career, including an Academy Award for Best Actress for her role in *Shakespeare in Love.* In 2008, she founded the lifestyle company Goop, which started as a newsletter and later expanded into a wellness and e-commerce brand. The company is known for promoting alternative wellness products and controversial health claims, which have attracted both supporters and critics.
5. Founded in 1988, **the Johns Hopkins Center for Health Security** is a research organization focusing on public health preparedness and response to emerging infectious diseases, pandemics, and other major health security challenges. The center conducts research, develops policies, and provides recommendations to governments, organizations, and individuals to enhance their readiness for public health emergencies. It also collaborates with various stakeholders, including government agencies, academic institutions, healthcare organizations, and international partners, to address global health security issues.

Remembering and Understanding

Activity 1 True or False Questions

Are the following statements true or false? Make your decisions based on the text.

(   ) 1. Online misinformation about COVID-19 is spreading slower than the virus itself.

Extensive Reading 3

( ) 2. The World Health Organization (WHO) has referred to the abundance of information about COVID-19 as an "infodemic".

( ) 3. A vaccine and a cure are currently available for COVID-19.

( ) 4. Drinking boiled garlic water can cure COVID-19.

( ) 5. Adding vitamin C supplements to your daily routine can prevent COVID-19.

( ) 6. Miracle Mineral Solutions (MMS) have been proven to be effective in treating cancer, HIV, autism, and coronavirus.

( ) 7. Individuals who spread false information about COVID-19 are primarily motivated by monetary gain.

( ) 8. Social media platforms like Twitter, Facebook, and Google are taking steps to remove false claims and promote accurate information about COVID-19.

( ) 9. The Internet has been used by the WHO and scientists to counter misinformation and share messages about protective measures for COVID-19.

( ) 10. Social media filters and algorithms are effective in tackling misinformation about COVID-19 and breaking through social media echo chambers.

Activity 2 Summarize the Text

What is the essay mainly about? Fill in the blanks with appropriate words to get a brief summary.

The spread of misinformation about COVID-19 is a significant problem, with false claims about the virus's (1)_____ spreading rapidly. This "infodemic" (2)_____ people's ability to find reliable information and guidance. Quacks and opportunists take advantage of this situation by spreading unverified information and (3)_____ online. Claims such as boiled garlic water or (4)_____ as cures for COVID-19 are not true, and relying on them can undermine containment efforts. (5)_____ like Miracle Mineral Solutions are also promoted as cures. Many individuals spread false information for (6)_____, while social media platforms and technology companies work to remove false claims and promote (7)_____. However, (8)_____ remains a challenge in combating misinformation. Collaboration between various stakeholders is necessary to ensure access to reliable and trustworthy information about COVID-19.

Reasoning and Analyzing

1. Why is online misinformation about COVID-19 referred to as an "infodemic" by the World Health Organization? What accounts for the infodemic?

_____

_____

2. Why is the overabundance of information about COVID-19 problematic?

3. What risks are associated with relying on alternative remedies and false claims about COVID-19?

4. Why do opportunists spread false information and sell dubious health products online during a pandemic?

5. What do Sather, Rivera, and Jim Bakker have in common? Why are they mentioned in Para. 8?

6. How can social media platforms and search engines contribute to combating misinformation about COVID-19?

7. "The Internet can also be an ally in the fight against infectious diseases." (Para. 10) Why does the author use "also" here?

8. What is an echo chamber? How are the social media echo chambers formed? Why will penetrating the social media echo chambers fueled by distrust in experts and news outlets be the real challenge in the fight against online misinformation about the coronavirus?

Reflecting and Creating

Activity 1 Topics for Discussion and Writing

1. The author argues, "Ultimately, the old advertising adage 'money follows eyeballs' still applies in the age of online misinformation." (Para. 7) What does "money follows eyeballs" imply? Can you find more examples demonstrating "money follows eyeballs"? Do you think this adage still applies in the age of online misinformation?

2. In Para. 9, Tara Kirk Sell says she understands why some people might be more receptive to inexpensive home remedies during a health crisis as "there is less tendency to trust in experts, authority, mainstream

Extensive Reading 3

media and medicine when there aren't many answers available". Do you agree with her? Are there any other possible explanations for people's receptiveness? In your opinion, which groups of people might be more susceptible to misinformation? Why? Do some research and write a short passage responding to the above questions.

3. Share a social media post spreading false information in class. How should you evaluate the credibility of the information before sharing it further? Discuss this in small groups and provide three strategies that individuals can use to verify the accuracy of information they encounter online.

4. Work in small groups and design a public awareness campaign to educate people about the dangers of online misinformation.

Activity 2 Evaluate the Author's Argument

The essay addresses the issue of "infodemic", discussing the dangers of false claims and quack remedies, the motivations behind spreading misinformation, the efforts of organizations like WHO and social media platforms to combat it, and the challenges in penetrating social media echo chambers. In your opinion, how effective is the argument? Fill out the checklist.

Questions	Comments
1. Is the author's position on the issue clear, or is it vague in some way?	
2. Does the author offer sound reasons?	
3. Are the reasons relevant to the argument and logically presented as a line of reasoning?	
4. Is there sufficient evidence to support his point of view?	
5. Does the author introduce irrelevant material, thereby wandering from his purpose?	
6. Does the author recognize any opposing views, or is the writing overly narrow in its own perspective?	
7. Is the text internally consistent, or does it contain unexplained contradictions?	
8. Does the author display fairness or bias?	

Unit 1 Critical Reading: A General Introduction

Text B How Can We Learn to Reject Fake News in the Digital World?

Preparatory Work

Five Ways to Spot Disinformation on Your Social Media Feeds, Source: ABC News

Activity 1 Small Group Discussion

In the era of social media, the circulation of fake news has become a prevalent challenge. False information spreads rapidly across various platforms, fueled by the ease of sharing and the absence of strict fact-checking measures. Individuals with malicious intent or those seeking to manipulate public opinion create and disseminate sensationalized or misleading content.

Source: Blocking Fake News: Blockchain as a Digital Notary

Think about the following questions, share your stories, and exchange your views.

- Have you ever encountered fake news or misinformation online? If yes, briefly describe your experience.
- How do you typically determine the credibility of an online source or news article?
- Why do you think it's important to be able to identify fake news?

Extensive Reading 3

Activity 2 What Is Metaliteracy?

The prefix "meta-" derives from the Greek word "metá", which carries several meanings, including "beyond" "transcending", and "at a higher level". In various contexts, the prefix "meta-" is used to denote something that is self-referential, abstract, or about itself. It often implies a more comprehensive or overarching concept related to the root word. The specific connotation can vary depending on the field or discipline in which it is used. For example:

❖ **Metadata**: Data about data. It refers to information that describes other data, such as the title, author, and date of creation of a document.

❖ **Metacognition**: Thinking about thinking. It relates to the process of being aware of and monitoring one's own thoughts and cognitive processes.

❖ **Metaphysics**: Beyond the physical. It is a branch of philosophy dealing with fundamental questions about reality, existence, and the nature of being.

❖ **Metamorphosis**: Transformation beyond a previous form. It refers to a profound change or transformation, often associated with the development of an organism from one stage to another (e.g., caterpillar to butterfly).

So, what is **metaliteracy**? How is it different from traditional literacy and digital literacy? Fill in the following box with relevant information about them respectively.

Source: Metaliteracy—SHB

Traditional literacy	Digital literacy	Metaliteracy

Unit 1 Critical Reading: A General Introduction

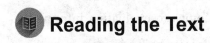 **Reading the Text**

> The rise of fake news on social media gained prominence in 2016 during the US presidential election, causing skepticism towards science, legitimate news, and societal norms. Its impact is increasingly evident in shaping societal values, influencing opinions on crucial issues, and challenging established facts, truths, and beliefs. While steps have been taken by some tech giants to address this issue, they fall short in tackling the pervasive problem of fake news. How can we learn to reject fake news in the digital world? Thomas P. Mackey and Trudi Jacobson have some insights.

How Can We Learn to Reject Fake News in the Digital World?

Thomas P. Mackey and Trudi Jacobson[1]

1 The circulation of fake news through social media in the 2016 presidential election has raised several concerns about online information.

2 Of course, there is nothing new about fake news as such—the satirical site "The Onion"[2] has long done this. Fake news satire is part of "Saturday Night Live"'s[3] Weekend Update and "The Daily Show"[4].

3 In these cases, the framework of humor is clear and explicit. That, however, is not the case in social media, which has emerged as a real news source. Pew Research Center reports that Facebook is "the most popular social media platform" and that "a majority of US adults—62 percent—get news on social media". When people read fake news on social media, they may be tricked into thinking they are reading real news.

4 Both Google and Facebook have promised to take measures to address the concerns of fake news masquerading as real news. A team of college students has already developed a browser plug-in called FiB to help readers identify on Facebook what is fake and what is real.

5 But these steps don't go far enough to address fake news.

6 The question then is: Can we better prepare ourselves to challenge and reject fabrications that may easily circulate as untruthful texts and images in the online world?

7 As scholars of library and information science, we argue that in today's complex world, traditional literacy, with its emphasis on reading and writing, and information literacy—the ability to search and retrieve information—are not enough.

8 What we need today is metaliteracy—an ability to make sense of the vast amounts of information in the connected world of social media.

9 Students today are consumers of the latest technology gadgets and social media platforms. However, they don't always have a deep understanding of the information transmitted through these devices, or how to be creators of online content.

10 Researchers at Stanford University recently found that "when it comes to evaluating information that flows through social media channels", today's "digital natives", despite being immersed in these environments, "are easily duped" by misinformation.

Digital literacy may not be enough. Digital devices image via www.shutterstock.com

11 They said they "were taken aback by students' lack of preparation" and argued that educators and policymakers must "demonstrate the link between digital literacy and citizenship".

12 The truth is that we live in a world where information lacks traditional editorial mechanisms of filter. It also comes in various styles and forms—it could range from digital images to multimedia to blogs and wikis. The veracity of all this information is not easily understood.

13 This problem has been around for a while. In 2005, for example, a false story about a political figure, John Seigenthaler Sr.[5], was posted by an anonymous author on Wikipedia, implicating him in the assassinations of President John F. Kennedy and Bobby Kennedy. Seigenthaler challenged this fake entry and it was eventually corrected. Several other hoaxes have circulated on Wikipedia over the years, showing how easy it is to post false information online.

14 Indeed, FactCheck.org is a website that monitors the accuracy of what is said by major US political players. In 2016, FactCheck.org published a set of practical steps to encourage closer reading and critical thinking.

15 As we see it, metaliteracy is a way to achieve these goals.

16 Digital literacy supports the effective use of digital technologies, while metaliteracy emphasizes how we think about things. Metaliterate individuals learn to reflect on how they process information based on their feelings or beliefs.

17 To do that, first and foremost, metaliterates learn to question sources of information. For example, metaliterate individuals learn to carefully differentiate among multiple sites, both formal (such as *The New York Times* or *Associated Press*) and informal (a blog post or tweet).

Metaliterates learn to question the sources of information. Jon S, CC BY

¹⁸ They question the validity of information from any of these sources and do not privilege one over the other. Information presented on a formal TV news source, such as CNN or Fox News, for instance, may be just as inaccurate as someone's blog post. This involves understanding all sources of information.

¹⁹ Second, metaliterates learn to observe their feelings when reading a news item. We are less inclined to delve further when something affirms our beliefs. On the other hand, we are more inclined to fact-check or examine the source of the news when we don't agree with it. Thinking about our own thinking reminds us that we need to move beyond how we feel, and engage our cognitive faculties in doing a critical assessment. Metaliterates pause to think whether they believe something because it affirms their ideas.

²⁰ Metaliteracy helps us understand the context from which the news is arising, noting whether the information emanates from research or editorial commentary, distinguishing the value of formal and informal news sources and evaluating comments left by others.

²¹ By reflecting on the way we are thinking about a news story, for instance, we will be more apt to challenge our assumptions, ask good questions about what we are reading and actively seek additional information.

²² Consider the recent example of how fake news was put out through a single tweet and believed by thousands of readers online. Eric Tucker, a 35-year-old cofounder of a marketing company in Austin, Texas, tweeted that anti-Trump protesters were professionally organized and bused to Trump rallies. Despite having only 40 Twitter followers, this one individual managed to start a conspiracy theory. Thousands of people believed and forwarded the tweet.

²³ This example shows how easy it is to transmit information online to a wide audience, even if it is not accurate. The combination of word and image in this case was powerful and supported what many people already believed to be true. But it also showed a failure to ask critical questions within an online community with shared ideas or to challenge one's own beliefs with careful reflection. In other words, just because information is shared widely on social media, that does not mean it is true.

²⁴ Another emphasis of metaliteracy is understanding how information is packaged and delivered.

²⁵ Packaging can be examined on a number of fronts. One is the medium used—is it text, photograph,

video, cartoon, illustration or artwork? The other is how it is used—is the medium designed to appeal to our feelings? Does professional-looking design provide a level of credibility to the unsuspecting viewer?

Metaliterates learn how to discriminate between fake and real news. Hand image via www.shutterstock.com

26 Social media makes it easy to produce and distribute all kinds of digital content. We can all be photographers or digital storytellers using online tools for producing and packaging well-designed materials. This can be empowering.

27 But the same material can be used to create intentionally false messages with appealing design features. Metaliterates learn to distinguish between formal and informal sources of information that may have very different or nonexistent editorial checks and balances.

28 They learn to examine the packaging of content. They learn to recognize whether the seemingly professional design may be a façade for a bias or misinformation. Realnewsrightnow, for example, is a slickly designed site with attention-grabbing but often false headlines. The About page of the website might raise questions, but only if a reader's mindset is evaluative.

29 Because social media is interactive and collaborative, the metaliterate learner must know how to contribute responsibly as well.

30 Metaliterate individuals recognize there are ethical considerations involved when sharing information, such as the information must be accurate. But there is more. Metaliteracy asks that individuals understand on a mental and emotional level the potential impact of one's participation.

31 So, metaliterate individuals don't just post random thoughts that are not based on truth. They learn that in a public space they have a responsibility to be fair and accurate.

32 Schools need to urge students to ponder these questions. Students need to be made aware of these issues early on so that they learn how not to develop uncritical assumptions and actions as they use technology.

33 They need to understand that whether they are posting a tweet, blog, Facebook post or writing a response to others online, they need to think carefully about what they are saying.

34 While social media offers much promise for providing everyone with a voice, there is a disturbing downside to this revolution. It has enabled the sharing of misinformation and false news stories that radically

alter representations of reality.

(Source: *The Conversation*, December 6, 2016.)

Notes

1. **Thomas P. Mackey** is Professor of Arts and Media at SUNY Empire State College. **Trudi E. Jacobson**, Distinguished Librarian, was the Head of the Information Literacy Department at the University at Albany, retiring in 2022. They co-developed the concept of metaliteracy and co-authored the first book on metaliteracy entitled: *Metaliteracy: Reinventing Information Literacy to Empower Learners* (2014). They are recognized for their pioneering work in the field of information literacy and metaliteracy, particularly in the context of higher education.

2. **The Onion** is a well-known satirical news organization that publishes fictional stories and parodies of real news events. It was founded in 1988 as a print newspaper and later expanded to an online platform. The Onion's articles often employ irony, exaggeration, and humor to comment on various aspects of society, politics, and popular culture.

3. *Saturday Night Live* (SNL) is a long-running American sketch comedy and variety show that has been on the air since October 11, 1975. The format of "Saturday Night Live" consists of a series of live sketches performed by a cast of comedians, often featuring celebrity guest hosts and musical performances. The show is known for its satirical and humorous take on current events, popular culture, and politics.

4. **The Daily Show** is a long-running American late-night television program that combines news satire and comedy. The show first premiered in 1996 and has since become one of the most popular and influential political satire shows on television.

5. **John Seigenthaler Sr.** (1927—2014) was an American journalist, writer, and political figure. He began his career as a journalist at *The Nashville Tennessean* newspaper in 1949 and rose through the ranks and eventually became the editor, publisher, and CEO of the paper. He served as a special assistant to Attorney General Robert F. Kennedy from 1961 to 1964 and played a crucial role in the civil rights movement. He also worked as an administrative assistant to US Senator Albert Gore Sr. and later served as the founding editorial director of *USA Today*. Seigenthaler was known for his commitment to journalism ethics and integrity.

Remembering and Understanding

Activity 1 Outline the Text

How do the two authors develop their ideas? Fill in the blanks with appropriate words to get a structured outline of the text.

Extensive Reading 3

Introduction (Paras. 1-3):
■ Concerns about the circulation of (1) _____.
■ New challenges presented by (2) _____ as it is considered a real news source.
The need for metaliteracy in the digital age (Paras. 4-8):
■ Inadequacy of existing measures to address fake news.
■ Insufficiency of traditional literacy and (3) _____.
■ (4) _____ as a way to navigate the vast amounts of information in social media.
Why digital literacy falls short (Paras. 9-15):
■ Students' lack of preparation for and susceptibility to misinformation.
■ The importance of linking digital literacy and (5) _____.
■ Various challenges with information in the digital age: lack of traditional editorial filters, difficulty in discerning (6) _____ and the ease of posting false information online.
Characteristics of metaliteracy (Paras. 16-28):
■ Questioning (7) _____ of information.
■ Observing and reflecting on personal feelings and biases.
■ Understanding the context of the news.
■ Examining the (8) _____ of information.
The responsibility of metaliterate individuals (Paras. 29-31):
■ Recognizing (9) _____ in sharing information.
■ Being fair, accurate, and responsible contributors in online spaces.
How to become metaliterate (Paras. 32-33):
■ Early awareness and education on critical thinking and (10) _____ use.
■ Encouraging thoughtful and responsible online communication.
Conclusion (Para. 34):
■ The importance of metaliteracy in an era of misinformation.

Activity 2 Answer the Following Questions

1. In the digital age, where do most people get information?

_____

_____

2. What is the main concern raised about fake news in the context of social media?

_____

Unit 1 Critical Reading: A General Introduction

3. What measures have been taken to address fake news on social media, according to the text? Are they effective?
   _____
   _____

4. Who are the "digital natives" in the text, "today's 'digital natives', despite being immersed in these environments, 'are easily duped' by misinformation"?
   _____
   _____

5. What did researchers at Stanford University discover about the ability of "digital natives" to evaluate information on social media?
   _____
   _____

6. What does the false story about John Seigenthaler Sr. posted on Wikipedia in 2005 demonstrate?
   _____
   _____

7. What are some key aspects of metaliteracy mentioned in the text?
   _____
   _____

8. Why is understanding the packaging and delivery of information important in metaliteracy?
   _____
   _____

9. Considering metaliteracy, what ethical considerations are involved in sharing information on social media?
   _____
   _____

10. Why is it important for schools to address these issues with students early on?
    _____
    _____

Reasoning and Analyzing

Choose the best answer to the question from the four choices given based on the text.

1. Which of the following statements best describes the difference between fake news satire and fake news on social media?

Extensive Reading 3

    A. Fake news on social media is more humorous and entertaining.

    B. Fake news on social media is intentionally misleading readers.

    C. Fake news satire is more prevalent on social media than fake news masquerading as real news.

    D. Fake news satire has traditional editorial mechanisms.

2. Based on the text, what is metaliteracy?

    A. The ability to differentiate between formal and informal news sources.

    B. The capacity to critically evaluate and make sense of information in the connected world of social media.

    C. A type of digital literacy that emphasizes the effective use of technology.

    D. The skill to identify and reject fake news without critical thinking.

3. According to researchers at Stanford University mentioned in the text, why are today's "digital natives" easily duped by misinformation on social media?

    A. They lack access to reliable sources of information.

    B. They are not immersed in social media environments.

    C. They do not value the importance of digital literacy.

    D. They are not adequately prepared to evaluate information critically.

4. What does the text suggest regarding the credibility of information presented by formal news sources versus informal sources?

    A. Formal news sources are always more accurate and trustworthy.

    B. Informal sources are more likely to contain false information.

    C. Both formal and informal sources can be equally inaccurate.

    D. Data from informal sources should never be considered valid information.

5. How does metaliteracy contribute to critical thinking and reflection?

    A. By encouraging individuals to question their own beliefs and assumptions.

    B. By promoting emotional responses to news items for deeper engagement.

    C. By focusing on the medium used to deliver information.

    D. By distinguishing between formal and informal sources of information.

6. What is one of the ethical considerations mentioned in the text regarding sharing information on social media?

    A. Ensuring the information is visually appealing and well-designed.

    B. Including personal biases and opinions in the shared content.

    C. Being responsible for the accuracy of the information being shared.

    D. Avoiding any form of participation or contribution on social media platforms.

7. The author's attitude towards fake news on social media can be best described as _____.

    A. concerned   B. pessimistic   C. indifferent   D. sarcastic

8. The purpose of the passage is to _____.

    A. argue for the importance of traditional literacy in the digital age

    B. explain the historical origins of fake news

    C. advocate for the adoption of metaliteracy as a response to fake news

    D. provide examples of misinformation spread through social media

Reflecting and Creating

Topics for discussion, writing, and presentation.

1. Choose a news article from a social media platform and evaluate its credibility using the principles of metaliteracy mentioned in the text. Identify the sources, question the validity, and consider the context in which the news is presented. Then, write a short analysis of your evaluation, highlighting the strengths and weaknesses of the article's credibility.

2. Choose a specific social media platform (e.g., Weibo, WeChat, QQ, Bilibili, Zhihu). Create a set of guidelines or tips for responsible information sharing and posting on that platform. Consider factors such as accuracy, source verification, and ethical considerations. Present the guidelines to the class, and have a discussion on the importance of responsible content creation and sharing.

3. Research a recent case of fake news or misinformation that went viral on social media. Gather information from different sources, including mainstream news outlets, fact-checking websites, and social media discussions. Then, create an infographic or visual presentation summarizing the incident, highlighting how it spread, the impact it had, and the steps taken to debunk or address the false information.

Summary

Self-reflection

Fill out the checklist.

Area	Yes / No?	Notes / Comments
I know what critical reading is.		
I know the relationship between critical reading and critical thinking.		

Extensive Reading 3

(continued)

I know the difference between critical reading and reading.		
I know the different areas to consider when reading critically.		
I know some questions to ask about the author and sources.		
I know some questions to ask about the evidence used.		
I know some questions to ask about the assumptions and biases of the writer.		

Value Cultivation

Quotes Exploration: Translate the following quotes into English or Chinese and explain them in your own words.

1. 子曰:"学而不思则罔,思而不学则殆。"——孔子《论语·为政》

2. 循序而渐进,熟读而精思。——朱熹《朱子全书·读书之要》

3. "吾生也有涯,而知也无涯。"对学习的追求是无止境的,既需苦学,还应"善读"。一方面,读书要用"巧力",读得巧,读得实,读得深,懂得取舍,注重思考,不做书呆子,不让有害信息填充我们的头脑;另一方面,也不能把读书看得太容易,不求甚解,囫囵吞枣,抓不住实质,把握不住精髓。

—— 习近平《求知善读,贵耳重目》

4. Critical thinking is a desire to seek, patience to doubt, fondness to meditate, slowness to assert, readiness to consider, carefulness to dispose and set in order; and hatred for every kind of imposture.

— Francis Bacon

Further Reading

1. 《求知善读,贵耳重目》(习近平:《之江新语》)
2. "Of Studies" by Francis Bacon
3. "How Social Media Endangers Knowledge" by Hossein Derakhshan

Unit 2
Getting Started

Extensive Reading 3

Mastering Critical Reading

While reading critically is essential for study and in life, the ability does not come naturally. The first step toward critical reading is comprehension—understanding what the author is saying and catching the central message intended for the readers. To get correct comprehension efficiently, especially for long and complicated writing, we can rely on some strategies, especially previewing, outlining, summarizing, and annotating, which can help us get deeper into reading and thinking.

Previewing

Previewing is making use of the related information about the material—the author, title, table of contents, etc.—to get an overview of it before reading it closely. Previewing enables readers to get a sense of what to expect in the material and to decide how to read it.

To preview a reading material, we…

❖ see what we can learn from the author, title, subtitles, preface, table of contents, exercises, etc.

❖ skim to get an overview of the content and organization

❖ decide on how we should read it: fast or slow, by skimming or in detail, etc.

Outlining

Outlining is an especially helpful reading strategy for understanding the content and structure of a reading selection. It requires us to distinguish between the main ideas and the less important material, such as examples or descriptions, and to uncover the structure or, at least, determine the main ideas.

Outlining can be done in two ways:

❖ a paragraph-by-paragraph outline, in which we list the main idea of each paragraph

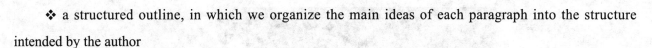

❖ a structured outline, in which we organize the main ideas of each paragraph into the structure intended by the author

To outline reading material, we…

❖ read the text for an overview of the content's structure

❖ identify the topic sentence, key phrases, and critical supporting details of each paragraph

❖ group topic sentences together by related ideas

❖ determine if supporting details describe a process or present an example, and which of these should be included in the outline

❖ arrange information according to levels and logically organize information using Roman numerals, capital letters, and Arabic numerals to represent the hierarchy of the levels

Enhancing Your Critical Reading (1)

Give a structured outline of Text A in Unit 1.

Summarizing

Writing a summary sets a higher requirement for us, one that goes beyond finding the main ideas and structure. We need to compose a condensed version of the text with all its major points in logical connections in our own words. Summarizing can be helpful in our understanding of the contents and, more importantly, in discovering the strengths and weaknesses of the piece.

Extensive Reading 3

Source: How to write a summary—BEST guide!

When writing a summary, we need to be fair, accurate, and complete. **To be more specific, we can check whether our summary is…**

- ❖ objective or neutral, which means we should present the original author's ideas only, not our own
- ❖ accurately expressed in our own words, and our language does not obscure the original ideas
- ❖ complete and balanced, giving proportionate coverage of original ideas
- ❖ smooth and coherent, standing alone as a unified piece of writing

💡 Enhancing Your Critical Reading (2)

Write a summary of Text B in Unit 1.

```
┌─────────────────────────────────────────────────────────────┐
│                                                             │
│                                                             │
│                                                             │
│                                                             │
│                                                             │
│                                                             │
│                                                             │
└─────────────────────────────────────────────────────────────┘
```

Annotating

Annotating means using various marks in the text or writing in the margin to note your reactions, appreciation, or confusion, thus recording your in-process understanding of the material. This strategy can be especially useful when you return to a text or review it later. It can not only remind you of your first impressions of the material, but also help you identify main points and come to new understandings.

To annotate while reading, we...

❖ Mark the text with different signs. For example, you can underline key words or sentences, bracket important sections of the text, use question marks or exclamation marks to note confusion or impressive points, connect ideas with lines or arrows, or number related points.

❖ Write notes in the margin. These notes may mention the main idea of a paragraph or section, questions about or responses toward some points, the structure of the material, the writing technique of the material, and any other things that strike you or impress you.

It is recommended that you annotate each time you read the material because you may have different understandings or reactions later, but use a different colored pen to differentiate new notes from previous annotations. Also, make your marks and notes brief and selective as too many things marked will reduce the significance of them all.

These strategies may not be sufficient in making our reading critical directly; however, they are the necessary preparation, getting us ready for the following analysis, evaluation, and reflection. What's more, they are useful for reading in general, not just for critical reading specifically.

Text A How to Mark a Book

Preparatory Work

Activity 1 Complete the Questionnaire

Answer the following questions to determine your preferences for and attitudes toward reading.

1. How many books (not textbooks) do you own?

Extensive Reading 3

2. How much time do you spend reading per day when it is your choice (not assigned in school)?

   A. I don't read unless I have to.

   B. Less than 30 minutes.

   C. Between 30 minutes and 1 hour.

   D. 1 hour or more.

3. Do you think you read enough?

   A. Yes.　B. No.

4. What do you choose to read (not for a school assignment)? Circle all choices that apply to you.

   A. Print Book.　　　　　　　B. E-Books.　　　　　　C. Magazines.

   D. Newspapers.　　　　　　E. Websites.　　　　　　F. Nothing.

5. What reading format do you prefer?

   A. Reading from a print book.

   B. Reading from an e-reader device (Kindle/Kobo/Nook, etc.).

   C. Reading from a computer.

   D. Reading from your smartphone.

   E. Reading from a tablet (Android/IPad/Microsoft Surface, etc.).

6. Where do you like reading? Indicate all choices that apply to you.

   A. In a library.

   B. In a dorm.

   C. In a classroom.

   D. In a canteen.

   Other (please specify) _____

7. What motivates you to read? Indicate all choices that apply to you.

   A. School assignments.

   B. Recommendation from a friend.

   C. Need for information for myself personally.

   D. Enjoyment.

   E. Relaxation.

   Other (please specify) _____

8. Do you prefer fiction or nonfiction?

   A. Fiction.　　B. Nonfiction.

9. How many books (not textbooks) do you read per year?

   A. More than ten books.

B. Five to ten books.

C. One to five books.

D. Zero.

10. **Do you check the background information of the author and the book before you start reading?**

    A. Yes.　　B. No.

11. **Do you annotate while reading?**

    A. Yes.　　B. No.

12. **If you were to recommend a book to your friends, you would choose _____.**

Activity 2 Explore Proper Names

Are you familiar with these proper names? Please find some background information about them to complete the table.

Proper names	Who he is / What it stands for
Mortimer Adler	
Paradise Lost	
Rembrandt	
Arturo Toscanini	
Brahms	
Gone with the Wind	
John Dewey	
Mr. Vallee	
Robert Hutchins	
Plutarch's Lives	
The Federalist Papers	

Extensive Reading 3

Reading the Text

> The conventional wisdom of "never marking up a book" has been advocated by countless teachers, librarians, and parents. However, Mortimer Adler holds a different perspective. According to Adler, if you personally own the book and are not concerned about preserving its physical appearance, marking it appropriately allows you to truly possess the book and integrate it into your own being.

How to Mark a Book

Mortimer Adler

1 You know you have to read "between the lines" to get the most out of anything. I want to persuade you to do something equally important in the course of your reading. I want to persuade you to write between the lines. Unless you do, you are not likely to do the most efficient kind of reading.

2 I contend, quite bluntly, that marking up a book is not an act of mutilation but of love.

3 You shouldn't mark up a book which isn't yours. Librarians (or your friends) who lend you books expect you to keep them clean, and you should. If you decide that I am right about the usefulness of marking books, you will have to buy them. Most of the world's great books are available today, in reprint editions.

4 There are two ways in which one can own a book. The first is the property right you establish by paying for it, just as you pay for clothes and furniture. But this act of purchase is only the prelude to possession. Full ownership comes only when you have made it a part of yourself, and the best way to make yourself a part of it is by writing in it. An illustration may make the point clear. You buy a beefsteak and transfer it from the butcher's icebox to your own. But you do not own the beefsteak in the most important sense until you consume it and get it into your bloodstream. I am arguing that books, too, must be absorbed in your bloodstream to do you any good.

5 Confusion about what it means to *own* a book leads people to a false reverence for paper, binding, and type—a respect for the physical thing—the craft of the printer rather than the genius of the author. They forget that it is possible for a man to acquire the idea, to possess the beauty, which a great book contains, without staking his claim by pasting his bookplate inside the cover. Having a fine library doesn't prove that its owner has a mind enriched by books; it proves nothing more than that he, his father, or his wife, was rich enough to buy them.

6 There are three kinds of book owners. The first has all the standard sets and best sellers—unread, untouched. (This deluded individual owns woodpulp and ink, not books.) The second has a great many books—a few of them read through, most of them dipped into, but all of them as clean and shiny as the day they were bought. (This person would probably like to make books his own, but is restrained by a false

respect for their physical appearance.) The third has a few books or many—every one of them dog-eared and dilapidated, shaken and loosened by continual use, marked and scribbled in from front to back. (This man owns books.)

7   Is it false respect, you may ask, to preserve intact and unblemished a beautifully printed book, an elegantly bound edition? Of course not. I'd no more scribble all over a first edition of *Paradise Lost* than I'd give my baby a set of crayons and an original Rembrandt! I wouldn't mark up a painting or a statue. Its soul, so to speak, is inseparable from its body. And the beauty of a rare edition or of a richly manufactured volume is like that of a painting or a statue.

8   But the soul of a book *can* be separate from its body. A book is more like the score of a piece of music than it is like a painting. No great musician confuses a symphony with the printed sheets of music. Arturo Toscanini reveres Brahms, but Toscanini's score of the C-minor Symphony is so thoroughly marked up that no one but the maestro himself can read it. The reason why a great conductor makes notations on his musical scores—marks them up again and again each time he returns to study them—is the reason why you should mark your books. If your respect for magnificent binding or typography gets in the way, buy yourself a cheap edition and pay your respects to the author.

9   Why is marking up a book indispensable to reading? First, it keeps you awake. (And I don't mean merely conscious; I mean wide awake.) In the second place, reading, if it is active, is thinking, and thinking tends to express itself in words, spoken or written. The marked book is usually the thought-through book. Finally, writing helps you remember the thoughts you had, or the thoughts the author expressed. Let me develop these three points.

10   If reading is to accomplish anything more than passing time, it must be active. You can't let your eyes glide across the lines of a book and come up with an understanding of what you have read. Now an ordinary piece of light fiction, like, say, *Gone with the Wind*, doesn't require the most active kind of reading. The books you read for pleasure can be read in a state of relaxation, and nothing is lost. But a great book, rich in ideas and beauty, a book that raises and tries to answer great fundamental questions, demands the most active reading of which you are capable. You don't absorb the ideas of John Dewey the way you absorb the crooning of Mr. Vallee. You have to reach for them. That you cannot do while you're asleep.

11   If, when you've finished reading a book, the pages are filled with your notes, you know that you read actively. The most famous "active" reader of great books I know is President Hutchins, of the University of Chicago. He also has the hardest schedule of business activities of any man I know. He invariably reads

Extensive Reading 3

with a pencil, and sometimes, when he picks up a book and pencil in the evening, he finds himself, instead of making intelligent notes, drawing what he calls "caviar factories" on the margins. When that happens, he puts the book down. He knows he's too tired to read, and he's just wasting time.

12 But, you may ask, why is writing necessary? Well, the physical act of writing, with your own hand, brings words and sentences more sharply before your mind and preserves them better in your memory. To set down your reaction to important words and sentences you have read, and the questions they have raised in your mind, is to preserve those reactions and sharpen those questions.

13 Even if you wrote on a scratch pad, and threw the paper away when you had finished writing, your grasp of the book would be surer. But you don't have to throw the paper away. The margins (top and bottom, as well as side), the end-papers, the very space between the lines, are all available. They aren't sacred. And, best of all, your marks and notes become an integral part of the book and stay there forever. You can pick up the book the following week or year, and there are all your points of agreement, disagreement, doubt, and inquiry. It's like resuming an interrupted conversation with the advantage of being able to pick up where you left off.

14 And that is exactly what reading a book should be: a conversation between you and the author. Presumably he knows more about the subject than you do; naturally, you'll have the proper humility as you approach him. But don't let anybody tell you that a reader is supposed to be solely on the receiving end. Understanding is a two-way operation; learning doesn't consist in being an empty receptacle. The learner has to question himself and question the teacher. He even has to argue with the teacher, once he understands what the teacher is saying. And marking a book is literally an expression of differences, or agreements of opinion, with the author.

Source: Annotating Readings with Hypothesis)

15 There are all kinds of devices for marking a book intelligently and fruitfully. Here's the way I do it:

- *Underlining*: of major points, of important or forceful statements.
- *Vertical lines at the margin*: to emphasize a statement already underlined.
- *Star, asterisk, or other doo-dad at the margin*: to be used sparingly, to emphasize the ten or twenty most important statements in the book. (You may want to fold the bottom corner of each

page on which you use such marks. It won't hurt the sturdy paper on which most modern books are printed, and you will be able to take the book off the shelf at any time and, by opening it at the folded-corner page, refresh your recollection of the book.)

■ *Numbers in the margin*: to indicate the sequence of points the author makes in developing a single argument.

■ *Numbers of other pages in the margin*: to indicate where else in the book the author made points relevant to the point marked; to tie up the ideas in a book, which, though they may be separated by many pages, belong together.

■ *Circling of key words or phrases*.

■ *Writing in the margin, or at the top or bottom of the page, for the sake of*: recording questions (and perhaps answers) which a passage raised in your mind; reducing a complicated discussion to a simple statement; recording the sequence of major points right through the books. I use the end-papers at the back of the book to make a personal index of the author's points in the order of their appearance.

16 The front end-papers are, to me, the most important. Some people reserve them for a fancy bookplate. I reserve them for fancy thinking. After I have finished reading the book and making my personal index on the back end-papers, I turn to the front and try to outline the book, not page by page or point by point (I've already done that at the back), but as an integrated structure, with a basic unity and an order of parts. This outline is, to me, the measure of my understanding of the work.

17 If you're a die-hard anti-book-marker, you may object that the margins, the space between the lines, and the end-papers don't give you room enough. All right. How about using a scratch pad slightly smaller than the page-size of the book—so that the edges of the sheets won't protrude? Make your index, outlines and even your notes on the pad, and then insert these sheets permanently inside the front and back covers of the book.

18 Or, you may say that this business of marking books is going to slow up your reading. It probably will. That's one of the reasons for doing it. Most of us have been taken in by the notion that speed of reading is a measure of our intelligence. There is no such thing as the right speed for intelligent reading. Some things should be read quickly and effortlessly and some should be read slowly and even laboriously. The sign of intelligence in reading is the ability to read different things differently according to their worth. In the case of good books, the point is not to see how many of them you can get through, but rather how many can get through you—how many you can make your own. A few friends are better than a thousand acquaintances. If this is your aim, as it should be, you will not be impatient if it takes more time and effort to read a great book than it does a newspaper.

19 You may have one final objection to marking books. You can't lend them to your friends because

Extensive Reading 3

nobody else can read them without being distracted by your notes. Furthermore, you won't want to lend them because a marked copy is a kind of intellectual diary, and lending it is almost like giving your mind away.

[20] If your friend wishes to read your *Plutarch's Lives*, Shakespeare, or *The Federalist Papers*, tell him gently but firmly, to buy a copy. You will lend him your car or your coat—but your books are as much a part of you as your head or your heart.

(Source: *The Saturday Review of Literature* on July 6, 1941.)

 Remembering and Understanding

Activity 1 Outline the Main Ideas

What does the author argue in the essay? How does he organize his ideas? Complete the following diagram by filling in the blanks.

Thesis
The most (1)_____ kind of reading is (2)_____ a book of (3)_____.

⬇

How to establish (4)_____ over books
There are two ways of (5)_____ and three kinds of (6)_____.

⬇

(7)_____ to mark a book
Marking up a book is (8)_____ to reading.

⬇

How to mark a book
There are all kinds of (9)_____ for marking a book (10)_____ and (11)_____.

⬇

(12) _____
People who don't like the idea are advised to develop the habit of marking up a book while reading.

Unit 2 Getting Started

Activity 2 Summarize the Text

What is the essay mainly about? Fill in the blanks with appropriate words to get a brief summary of it.

Mortimer Adler tells us to (1)"_____" in order to do the most efficient kind of reading. He claims that you don't truly own the books unless (2)_____, and (3)_____ is the best way to make it become yours. Marking up a book is indispensable because it keeps you (4)_____. We may record our thoughts, which are the results of active reading, and the physical act of writing will (5)_____. Adler explains how to mark up a book by (6)_____, including underlining, (7)_____, and writing responses in the margins. Adler addresses (8)_____ that people come up with to avoid active reading and marking their books.

Activity 3 Identify and Synthesize Information

In the essay, Adler argues that "writing between the lines" is indispensable if "reading is to accomplish anything more than passing time". What are the benefits of writing in a book? What books cannot be marked?

Benefits of marking up a book
1. It keeps one _____.
2. It represents _____, that is, thinking while reading.
3. It helps one remember the _____ they have done.
4. Writing improves _____ (helps bring _____ more sharply before your mind and _____ them better.)
5. Writing helps preserve your reactions and _____.
6. It can make it possible for you to _____ where you left off.
7. It indicates one has conducted _____ with the author.

Books that cannot be marked
1. Books _____
2. Books _____
3. Books _____
4. Books _____

Extensive Reading 3

Reasoning and Analyzing

Answer the following questions.

1. Adler argues that unless you "write between the line", "you are not likely to do the most efficient kind of reading". What does he mean by "the most efficient kind of reading"?

   _____
   _____

2. Why does Adler mention the purchase of a beefsteak?

   _____
   _____

3. There are three kinds of book owners, according to the author. How does he classify them into the three kinds, or what is the criterion for his classification?

   _____
   _____

4. Why does Adler refer to Arturo Toscanini's score of Brahms's C Minor Symphony?

   _____
   _____

5. "You don't absorb the ideas of John Dewey the way you absorb the crooning of Mr. Vallee." What's the difference between John Dewey and Mr. Vallee? What's the purpose of the author in this comparison?

   _____
   _____

6. What does the example of President Hutchins demonstrate?

   _____
   _____

7. Why does Adler think reading a book is somewhat like having a conversation with the author?

   _____
   _____

8. Does the author recognize any opposing ideas? If so, what are the different views, and how does he respond to them?

   _____
   _____

Reflecting and Creating

Activity 1 Topics for Discussion and Writing

1. Adler shares his own devices for marking up a book in the essay. Which ones do you use on a regular basis? Which ones might help you in your study? Which devices are you unlikely to try? Give your explanations.
2. Adler contends that marking up a book is not an act of mutilation but of love, and it's improper to refuse to write in books while reading. Do you think he is right? Write a paragraph answer to his question.
3. The author thinks the soul of a book can be separated from its body. Do you side with him? Give your explanations.
4. What is the writer's attitude toward lending books? Do you share his attitude? Why or why not?
5. Suppose your friend never marks in a book. Write a short passage to persuade them to write between the lines when they are reading.

Activity 2 Evaluate the Author's Argument

How much do you agree with the author that "writing between the lines" is the most efficient kind of reading? Fill out the checklist.

Questions	Comments
1. Is the author's position on the issue clear, or is it vague in some way?	
2. Does the author offer sound reasons?	
3. Are the reasons relevant to the argument and logically presented as a line of reasoning?	
4. Is there sufficient evidence to support his point of view?	
5. Does the author introduce irrelevant material, thereby wandering from his purpose?	
6. Does the author recognize any opposing views, or is the writing overly narrow in its own perspective?	
7. Is the text internally consistent, or does it contain unexplained contradictions?	
8. Does the author display fairness or bias?	

Extensive Reading 3

Text B How Come the Quantum

Preparatory Work

Source: What Is Quantum Entanglement?, *IEEE Spectrum*

Have you ever wondered how the world came into being? Why do things exist? What is a "black hole"? How much do you know about quantum phenomena? Please share your answer to these questions and your predictions about the content of this article.

What I know about the topic	What I predict the article is writing about

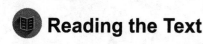

Reading the Text

> How did the world come into being? Why do things exist? What is the greatest mystery in physics today? John Archibald Wheeler tries to find the answers to the above in another question—how come the quantum? For over a century, physicists have grappled with understanding the fundamental properties and behaviors of quantum phenomena. As scientists continue to explore the intricacies of the quantum universe, the quest for understanding "how come the quantum" remains one of the most profound and elusive questions in the realm of physics.

How Come the Quantum

John Archibald Wheeler[1]

1   What is the greatest mystery in physics today? Different physicists have different answers. My candidate for greatest mystery is a question now a century old, "How come the quantum?" What is this thing, the "quantum"? It's a bundle of energy, an indivisible unit that can be sliced no more. Max Planck[2] showed us a hundred years ago that light is emitted not in a smooth, steady flow, but in quanta. Then physicists found quantum jumps of energy, the quantum of electric charge and more. In the small-scale world, everything is lumpy.

2   And more than just lumpy. When events are examined closely enough, uncertainty prevails; cause and effect become disconnected. Change occurs in little explosions in which matter is created and destroyed, in which chance guides what happens, in which waves are particles and particles are waves.

3   Despite all this uncertainty, quantum physics is both a practical tool and the basis of our understanding of much of the physical world. It has explained the structure of atoms and molecules, the thermonuclear burning that lights the stars, the behavior of semiconductors and superconductors, the radioactivity that heats the earth, and the comings and goings of particles from neutrinos to quarks.

4   Successful, yes, but mysterious, too. Balancing the glory of quantum achievements, we have the shame of not knowing "how come". Why does the quantum exist?

5   My mentor, the Danish physicist Niels Bohr[3], made his peace with the quantum. His "Copenhagen interpretation"[4] promulgated in 1927 bridged the gap between the strangeness of the quantum world and the ordinariness of the world around us. It is the act of measurement, said Bohr, that transforms the indefiniteness of quantum events into the definiteness of everyday experience. And what one can measure, he said, is necessarily limited. According to his principle of complementarity, you can look at something in one way or in another way, but not in both ways at once. It may be, as one French physicist put it, "the fog from the north", but the Copenhagen interpretation remains the best interpretation of the quantum that we have.

Extensive Reading 3

Source: Niels Bohr Institute: "Planets in the habitable zone around most stars, calculate researchers"

6 Albert Einstein, for one, could never accept this world view. In on-again, off-again debates over more than a dozen years, Bohr and Einstein argued the issues — always in a spirit of great mutual admiration and respect. I made my own effort to convince Einstein, but without success. Once, around 1942, I went around to his house in Princeton to tell him of a new way of looking at the quantum world developed by my student, Richard Feynman.[5]

7 Feynman pictured an electron getting from point A to point B not by one or another possible path, but by taking all possible paths at once. Einstein, after listening patiently, said, as he had on other occasions, "I still cannot believe God plays dice."[6] Then he added, "But maybe I have earned the right to make my mistakes."

Source: What Einstein Actually Thought of Quantum Mechanics

8 Feynman's superposed paths are eerie enough. In the 1970s, I got interested in another way to reveal the strangeness of the quantum world. I called it "delayed choice". You send a quantum of light (a photon) into an apparatus that offers the photon two paths. If you measure the photon that leaves the apparatus in one way, you can tell which path it took.

9 If you measure the departing photon in a different way (a complementary way), you can tell if it took both paths at once. You can't make both kinds of measurements on the same photon, but you can decide, after the photon has entered the apparatus, which kind of measurement you want to make.

10 Is the photon already wending its way through the apparatus along the first path? Too bad. You decide to look to see if it took both paths at once, and you find that it did. Or is it progressing along both paths at once? Too bad. You decide to find out if it took just one path, and it did.

11 At the University of Maryland, Carroll Alley, with Oleg Jakubowicz and William Wickes, took up the challenge I offered them and confirmed that the outcome could be affected by delaying the choice of measurement technique — the choice of question asked — until the photon was well on its way. I like to think that we may one day conduct a delayed-choice experiment not just in a laboratory, but in the cosmos.

12 One hundred years is, after all, not so long a time for the underpinning of a wonderfully successful theory to remain murky. Consider gravity. Isaac Newton, when he published his monumental work on gravitation in the 17th century, knew he could not answer the question, "How come gravity?" He was wise enough not to try. "I frame no hypotheses," he said.

13 It was 228 years later when Einstein, in his theory of general relativity, attributed gravity to the curvature of space-time. The essence of Einstein's lesson can be summed up with the aphorism, "Mass tells space-time how to curve, and space-time tells mass how to move." Even that may not be the final answer. After all, gravity and the quantum have yet to be joined harmoniously.

Photo: The Garden of Academe, The Holbarn Archive / Bridgeman Images

14 On the windowsill of my home on an island in Maine I keep a rock from the garden of Academe,[7] a rock that heard the words of Plato and Aristotle as they walked and talked. Will there someday arise an equivalent to that garden where a few thoughtful colleagues will see how to put it all together and save us from the shame of not knowing "how come the quantum"? Of course, in this century, that garden will be as large as the earth itself, a "virtual" garden where the members of my imagined academy will stroll and converse electronically.

15 Here, a hundred years after Planck, is quantum physics, the intellectual foundation for all of chemistry, for biology, for computer technology, for astronomy and cosmology. Yet, proud foundation for so much, it does not yet know the foundation for its own teachings. One can believe, and I do believe, that the answer to

Extensive Reading 3

the question, "How come the quantum?" will prove to be also the answer to another question, "How come existence?"

(Source: The *New York Times*, December, 2000.)

Notes

1. **John Archibald Wheeler** (1911—2008), professor of physics at Princeton University, was largely responsible for reviving interest in general relativity in the US after World War II and is best known for popularizing the term "black hole".

2. **Max Karl Ernst Ludwig Planck** (1858—1947) was a German physicist who is considered the founder of quantum theory. Planck is best known for introducing the concept of quantization of energy, which revolutionized our understanding of the behavior of energy and matter at the atomic and subatomic levels. His work laid the foundation for modern physics and earned him the Nobel Prize in Physics in 1918.

3. **Niels Henrik David Bohr** (1885—1962) was a Danish physicist who made significant contributions to the understanding of atomic structure and quantum mechanics. For his groundbreaking work in physics, Niels Bohr was awarded the Nobel Prize in Physics in 1922.

4. **The Copenhagen interpretation** is a foundational interpretation of quantum mechanics, named after the city where it was formulated at the Solvay Conference in 1927. It was proposed by Niels Bohr and Werner Heisenberg, among others.

5. **Richard Phillips Feynman** (1918—1988) was an American physicist known for his exceptional contributions to theoretical physics, particularly in the fields of quantum mechanics and quantum electrodynamics, for which he was awarded the Nobel Prize in Physics in 1965.

6. Einstein preferred a deterministic view of physics and sought a more complete theory that would explain quantum phenomena without inherent uncertainty. He believed in a more fundamental order underlying the universe and expressed his skepticism by using the metaphor of **God playing dice**.

Remembering and Understanding

Activity 1 Multiple-choice Questions

Choose the best answer from the four choices given based on the text.

1. According to the passage, the "greatest mystery" in physics today is _____.

    A. the origin of gravity

    B. the behavior of particles in the small-scale world

    C. the connection between gravity and the quantum

    D. the uncertainty and lumpy nature of the quantum world

Unit 2 Getting Started

2. What did Niels Bohr propose in his "Copenhagen interpretation"?

   A. The measurement of quantum events transforms them into everyday experiences.

   B. Quantum events can be observed in multiple ways simultaneously.

   C. The quantum world is incomprehensible and cannot be understood.

   D. The existence of quanta is the fundamental building block of reality.

3. In the passage, Einstein expresses his disagreement with _____.

   A. the existence of quanta

   B. the Copenhagen interpretation

   C. the uncertainty principle

   D. the behavior of electrons in Feynman's theory

4. What is delayed choice?

   A. A method to measure the behavior of electrons in Feynman's theory.

   B. A technique to analyze quantum events after they have occurred.

   C. The choice of how to measure a quantum event made after the event has started.

   D. An experiment that demonstrates the strange behavior of photons in different measurement setups.

5. What is the main point the author is trying to convey in this passage?

   A. The quantum world is inherently mysterious and may never be fully understood.

   B. The foundation of quantum physics remains uncertain, but great progress is being made.

   C. Quantum physics has practical applications but lacks a clear explanation for the enigmatic nature of the quantum world.

   D. Studying the quantum world has led to significant advancements in various fields.

Activity 2 Summarize the Text

Write a summary of the text based on your answers to the questions above.

```
┌─────────────────────────────────────────────────────────┐
│                                                         │
│                                                         │
│                                                         │
│                                                         │
│                                                         │
└─────────────────────────────────────────────────────────┘
```

Reasoning and Analyzing

Answer the following questions.

1. How did Niels Bohr explain the transformation of quantum events into everyday experience?

   _____

Extensive Reading 3

2. Why could Albert Einstein not accept the Copenhagen interpretation?
   _____
   _____

3. What was Richard Feynman's perspective on the quantum world?
   _____
   _____

4. What did Carroll Alley, Oleg Jakubowicz, and William Wickes confirm through their analysis?
   _____
   _____

5. Why does the author mention Newton's approach to gravity in Para. 12?
   _____
   _____

6. What is the author's perspective on the future of understanding the quantum?
   _____
   _____

7. According to the author, what might be the answer to both "How come the quantum?" and "How come existence?"?
   _____
   _____

8. What does the author hope for in the realm of quantum physics?
   _____
   _____

✈ Reflecting and Creating

Compare your annotations with the ones below and have a discussion based on the following questions.

❖ What devices are used respectively in the annotations to the article?
❖ Do the annotations help you understand the article better? If yes, in what ways? If not, why not?
❖ Is there anything to be improved in the annotations?

SAMPLE ANNOTATED TEXT

"How Come the Quantum"

By John Archibald Wheeler

Bold = Main Ideas Universal Font = Descriptive Outline *Italics = Comments*

intro of topic

What is the greatest mystery in physics today? Different physicists have different answers. My candidate for greatest mystery is a question now century old, "How come the quantum?" What is this thing, the "quantum"? It's a bundle of energy, an indivisible unit that can be sliced no more. Max Planck showed us a hundred years ago that light is emitted not in a smooth, steady flow, but in quanta. Then physicists found quantum jumps of energy, the quantum of electric charge and more. In the small-scale world, everything is lumpy.

Greatest mystery in physics is nature of quantum.

historical perspective

lumps of energy?

description

And more than just lumpy. When events are examined closely enough, uncertainty prevails; cause and effect become disconnected. Change occurs in little explosions in which matter is created and destroyed, in which chance guides what happens, in which waves are particles and particles are waves.

chance plays great role in change in this "small scale world"

This means they're the same and different at the same time?

main idea of essay

Despite all this uncertainty, quantum physics is both a practical tool and the basis of our understanding of much of the physical world. It has explained the structure of atoms and molecules, the thermonuclear burning that lights the stars, the behavior of semiconductors and superconductors, the radioactivity that heats the earth, and the comings and goings of particles from neutrinos to quarks.

quantum physics has helped us understand material world

both what things are and how they work

rhetorical question

Successful, yes, but mysterious, too. Balancing the glory of quantum achievements, we have the shame of not knowing "how come." Why does the quantum exist?

some things remains a mystery
Science can't tell us why anything exists. We still need religion for that.

one interpretation

My mentor, the Danish physicist, Niels Bohr, made his peace with the quantum. His "Copenhagen Interpretation" promulgated in 1927 bridged the gap between the strangeness of the quantum world and the ordinariness of the world around us. It is the act of measurement, said Bohr, that transforms the indefiniteness of quantum events into the definiteness of everyday experience.

Bohr suggested it's measurement that makes the quantum useful

Its mysterious quality is a separate issue.

Extensive Reading 3

	And what one can measure, he said, is necessarily limited. According to his principle of complementarity, you can look at something in one way or in another way, but not in both ways at once. It may be, as one French physicist put it, "the fog from the north," but the Copenhagen interpretation remains the best interpretation of the quantum that we have.	This is best theory we have.
anecdote	Albert Einstein, for one, could never accept this world view. In on-again, off-again debates over more than a dozen years, Bohr and Einstein argued the issues–always in a spirit of great mutual admiration and respect. I made my own effort to convince Einstein, but without success. Once, around 1942, I went around to his house in Princeton to tell him of a new way of looking at the quantum world developed by my student, Richard Feynman.	Einstein didn't accept this

I'm with Einstein on this.

name-dropper! |
| second interpretation | Feynman pictured an electron getting from point A to point B not by one or another possible path, but by taking all possible paths at once. Einstein, after listening patiently, said, as he had on other occasions, "I still cannot believe God plays dice." Then he added, "But maybe I have earned the right to make my mistakes." | Feynman proposed another explanation.

Einstein recognizing the limits of science? |
| third interpretation | Feynman's superposed paths are eerie enough. In the 1970s, I got interested in another way to reveal the strangeness of the quantum world. I called it "delayed choice." You send a quantum of light (a photon) into an apparatus that offers the photon two paths. If you measure the photon that leaves the apparatus in one way you can tell which path it took. | Another explanation is "delayed choice." |
| explanation of third interpretation | If you measure the departing photon in a different way (a complementary way), you can tell if it took both paths at once. You can't make both kinds of measurements on the same photon, but you can decide, after the photon has entered the apparatus, which kind of measurement you want to make. | You can look at 2 measurements, but not both at once. |
| explanation, continued

This makes no sense. What's too bad? | Is the photon already wending its way through the apparatus along the first path? Too bad. You decide to look to see if it took both paths at once, and you find that it did. Or is it progressing along both paths at once? Too bad. You decide to find out if it took just one path, and it did. | Your "delayed choice" of how to measure influences the outcome. |

Unit 2 Getting Started

anecdote

But does a lab have anything to do with the "real" cosmos?

At the University of Maryland, Carroll Alley, with Oleg Jakubowicz and William Wickes, took up the challenge I offered them and confirmed that the outcome could be affected by delaying the choice of measurement technique–the choice of question asked–until the photon was well on its way. I like to think that <u>we may one day conduct a delayed-choice experiment not just in a laboratory, but in the cosmos.</u>

theory confirmed in lab; may be confirmed in cosmos some day

Analogy

<u>One hundred years is, after all, not so long a time for the underpinning of a wonderfully successful theory to remain murky. Consider gravity.</u> Isaac Newton, when he published his monumental work on gravitation in the 17th century, knew he could not answer the question, "How come gravity?" He was wise enough not to try. "I frame no hypotheses," he said.

The "why" of gravity was a mystery at first, too.

development of analogy

It was 228 years later [that] Einstein, in his theory of general relativity, attributed gravity to the curvature of space-time. The essence of Einstein's lesson can be summed up with the aphorism, "<u>Mass tells space-time how to curve, and space-time tells mass how to move.</u>" Even that may not be the final answer. After all, gravity and the quantum have yet to be joined harmoniously.

Einstein explained the "why" of gravity, but even that may not be the final word.

That's a description, not an explanation.

speculation

On the windowsill of my home on an island in Maine, I keep a rock from the garden of Academe, a rock that heard the words of Plato and Aristotle as they walked and talked. Will there someday arise an equivalent to that garden where a few thoughtful colleagues will see how to put it all together and save us from the shame of not knowing "how come the quantum"? Of course, in this century, that garden will be as large as the earth itself, <u>a "virtual" garden</u> where the members of my imagined academy will stroll and converse electronically.

Perhaps physicists will one day solve the "why" of the quantum.

nice reference to the Internet

conclusion

Here, a hundred years after Planck, is quantum physics, the intellectual foundation for all of chemistry, for biology, for computer technology, for astronomy and cosmology. Yet, proud foundation for so much, it does not yet know the foundation for its own teachings. One can believe, and I do believe, that <u>the answer to the question, "How come the quantum?" will prove to be also the answer to another question, "How come existence?"</u>

quantum physics, foundation for so many fields, is itself built on a mystery

He thinks we can understand meaning through science—a purely descriptive field.

Credit: Dr. Murray and Anna C. Rockowitz Writing Center, Hunter College, City University of New York

Extensive Reading 3

Summary

💡 Self-reflection

Fill out the checklist.

Area	Yes / No?	Notes / Comments
I know the importance of previewing, outlining, summarizing, and annotating in critical reading.		
I know how to preview, outline, and summarize a text.		
I know when (not) to annotate while reading.		
I know how to annotate a text/book by highlighting and writing.		
I can get deeper into a text/book with annotations.		
I find annotations help me reflect on the text/book more effectively.		

👤 Value Cultivation

Match the quotes with the people who said them, shown below. Please note that there are two extra options you do not need to use. Translate the quotes into English or Chinese and explain them in your own words.

1. 博学而笃志，切问而近思，仁在其中矣。
2. 绩学之士，读书必有剳记，以记所得著所疑。记所得则要领明矣，著所疑则启他日读书参证之途矣。
3. Books give a soul to the universe, wings to the mind, flight to the imagination, and life to everything.
4. To utter protest, or approval, or question or correct or in any way assault the book with a pencil, you must agree that the love of annotating books is one of the most permanent and rigorous pastimes in the human mind.
5. The reading of all good books is like a conversation with the finest minds of past centuries.

    A. 孔子   B. 子夏   C. 徐特立   D. Albert Einstein

    E. Rene Descartes   F. Virginia Woolf   G. Plato

_____
_____
_____
_____
_____

📖 Further Reading

1. 《读书的艺术》（林语堂，1931）
2. "On Reading" by W. Somerset Maugham (1939)
3. "A Brief Note in the Margin: Virginia Woolf and Annotating" by Amanda Golden (2012)

Unit 3
Learning to Ask Questions

Mastering Critical Reading

"Questioning lies at the heart of comprehension because it is the process of questioning, seeking answers, and asking further questions that keeps the reading going" (Harvey). To become critical readers, we need to engage with texts by using different types of questioning. This form of questioning can be used to explore ideas, get to the root of things, uncover assumptions, analyze complex concepts, etc. Socrates, a Greek philosopher from Athens, is known for encouraging people to think carefully about ideas before accepting them and for developing the method of examining ideas according to a system of questions and answers to discover the truth. Therefore, learning to ask questions like Socrates is a natural place to start.

Source: Socratic Questioning for Idea Generation and Critical Thinking

■ **Socratic Questioning**

❖ **What is it?**

Named after the ancient Greek philosopher Socrates, who lived circa 400 BC, Socratic questioning is a process where questions are used to construct and examine knowledge and considered to be a vital part of the critical thinking process. Socratic questioning dives deep into fundamental concepts, principles, theories, issues, or problems with a systematic and disciplined approach.

❖ **Why is it important?**

The art of skillful Socratic questioning is designed to make the reader an active participant, rather than a passive recipient, in learning. It teaches us the difference between systematic and fragmented thinking. It teaches us to dig beneath the surface of our and others' ideas. Through the use of carefully constructed questions, we can interact with the text and the author, thereby thinking about the subject at hand from different angles in the quest for greater understanding and truth.

❖ **Types of Socratic Questions**

Based on R. W. Paul's classification, Socratic questions can be divided into the following types:

Socratic question type	Examples
Questions for clarification	What do you mean by…? Could you put that another way? What do you think is the main issue? Could you give us an example? Could you explain that further?
Questions that probe assumptions	What are you assuming? Why would you make this assumption? What could we assume instead? You seem to be assuming… How would you justify this for granted? Is that always the case?
Questions that probe reason and evidence	What would be an example? Why do you think this is true? What other information do we need to know before we can address this question? Could you explain your reason to us? By what reasoning did you come to that conclusion? Is there reason to doubt that evidence? What led you to that belief?
Questions of origin or source	Is this your idea or did you hear it from someplace else? Have you always felt this way? Has your opinion been influenced by something or someone? Where did you get that idea? What caused you to feel that way?
Questions that probe implications and consequences	What effect would that have? Could that really happen or probably happen? What is an alternative? What are you implying by that? If that happened, what else would happen as a result? Why?

Extensive Reading 3

(continued)

Questions about viewpoints or perspectives	Is there another way to look at this?
	How would other groups of people respond to this question? Why?
	How could you answer the objection that …would make?
	What are the arguments to the contrary, if any?
	How are … and …'s ideas alike? Different?
Questions about the question	Why is this question important?
	Is this question easy or difficult to answer?
	Why do you think that?
	What assumptions can we make based on this question?
	Does this question lead to other important issues and questions?

💡 Enhancing Your Critical Reading (3)

Source: Questioning in the Classroom: How to Improve Your Skills

The following is a questioning dialogue taking place between a teacher and her students on the discussion of global warming. Read it and identify the types of questions asked and examine how the teacher leads the students to understand global warming by questioning.

Teacher: What is happening to our global climate?

Stan: It's getting warmer.

Teacher: How do you know it's getting warmer? What evidence do you have to support your answer?

Stan: It's in the news all of the time. They are always saying that it's not as cold as it used to be. We have all of these record heat days.

Teacher: Has anyone else heard of this kind of news?

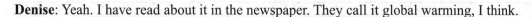

Denise: Yeah. I have read about it in the newspaper. They call it global warming, I think.

Teacher: Are you saying that you learned about global warming from newscasters? Are you assuming they know that global warming is occurring?

Heidi: I heard it too. It's terrible. The ice caps in the Arctic are melting. The animals are losing their homes. I think the newscasters hear it from the scientists that are studying the issue.

Teacher: If that is the case and the scientists are telling the newscasters, how do the scientists know?

Chris: They have instruments to measure climate. They conduct research that measures the Earth's temperature.

Teacher: How long do you think scientists have been doing this?

Grant: Probably 100 years.

Candace: Maybe a little more than that.

Teacher: Actually, it's been studied for about 140 years. Since about 1860.

Heidi: We were close.

Teacher: Yes. How did you know that?

Grant: I just figured that seems like when instruments were available and scientists had the means to measure climate like that.

Teacher: So, looking at the last 100 year's climate on this graph, what can we say about the Earth's climate?

Raja: The 20th century has become much warmer than previous centuries.

Teacher: Can we hypothesize why?

Raja: One word: pollution.

Teacher: What are you assuming when you say that pollution is the cause for the temperatures to rise?

Heidi: Carbon dioxide from cars causes pollution and chemicals from factories.

Frank: Hair spray causes dangerous chemicals to get into the atmosphere.

Teacher: Okay. Let's take a minute to review what we've discussed so far.

(Source: https://www.passeidireto.com/arquivo/122020536/dep-question-socratic)

Socratic question type	Questions asked by the teacher
1	What is happening to our global climate?
2	How do you know it's getting warmer?
3	What evidence do you have to support your answer?
4	Has anyone else heard of this kind of news?

Extensive Reading 3

(continued)

5	Are you saying that you learned about global warming from newscasters?
6	Are you assuming they know that global warming is occurring?
7	If that is the case and the scientists are telling the newscasters, how do the scientists know?
8	How long do you think scientists have been doing this?
9	How did you know that?
10	So, looking at the last 100 year's climate on this graph, what can we say about the Earth's climate?
11	Can we hypothesize why?
12	What are you assuming when you say that pollution is causing global temperatures to rise?

Text A The Man Who Asked Questions (Excerpt)

Preparatory Work

Activity 1 Learn to Ask Questions About the Title

Consider the title "The Man Who Asked Questions" and ask at least four questions about it.

Questions about the title
1. Who is the man?
2.
3.
4.
…

Activity 2 Watch a Video About Socrates

What do you know about the man who asked questions, Socrates? Try to write as much as possible about him in the space below and add relevant information after watching a short video.

Life	
Personality	
Teaching	
Philosophy	
Death	
Quotes	
Legacy	
opinion about him	

Reading the Text

Socrates, a Greek philosopher from Athens (470—399 BC), remains a highly significant figure in critical thinking and analysis. Despite never committing his ideas to writing and facing a fatal sentence due to his persistent questioning, his legacy endures as one of the most influential in history.

The Man Who Asked Questions (Excerpt)

Nigel Warburton[1]

1　About 2,400 years ago in Athens a man was put to death for asking too many questions. There were philosophers before him, but it was with Socrates that the subject really took off. If philosophy has a patron saint, it is Socrates.

2　Snub-nosed, podgy, shabby and a bit strange, Socrates did not fit in. Although physically ugly and often unwashed, he had great charisma and a brilliant mind. Everyone in Athens agreed that there had never been anyone quite like him and probably wouldn't be again. He was unique. But he was also extremely annoying. He saw himself as one of those horseflies that have a nasty bite—a gadfly. They're irritating, but don't do

Extensive Reading 3

serious harm. Not everyone in Athens agreed, though. Some loved him; others thought him a dangerous influence.

3   As a young man he had been a brave soldier fighting in the Peloponnesian Wars[2] against the Spartans and their allies. In middle age he shuffled around the marketplace, stopping people from time to time and asking them awkward questions. That was more or less all he did. But the questions he asked were razor-sharp. They seemed straightforward; but they weren't.

Source: Socrates and the Marketplace—Katherine Ketcham

4   An example of this was his conversation with Euthydemus[3]. Socrates asked him whether being deceitful counted as being immoral. Of course it does, Euthydemus replied. He thought that was obvious. But what, Socrates asked, if your friend is feeling very low and might kill himself, and you steal his knife? Isn't that a deceitful act? Of course it is. But isn't it moral rather than immoral to do that? It's a good thing, not a bad one—despite being a deceitful act. Yes, said Euthydemus, who by now is tied in knots. Socrates by using a clever counter-example has shown that Euthydemus' general comment that being deceitful is immoral doesn't apply in every situation. Euthydemus hadn't realized this before.

5   Over and over again Socrates demonstrated that the people he met in the marketplace didn't really know what they thought they knew. A military commander would begin a conversation totally confident that he knew what "courage" meant, but after 20 minutes in Socrates' company would leave completely confused. The experience must have been disconcerting. Socrates loved to reveal the limits of what people genuinely understood, and to question the assumptions on which they built their lives. A conversation that ended in everyone realizing how little they knew was for him a success. Far better that than to carry on believing that you understood something when you didn't.

Socrates teaching Perikles, by Nicolas Guibal, 1780

Unit 3 Learning to Ask Questions

6   At that time in Athens the sons of rich men would be sent to study with Sophists[4]. The Sophists were clever teachers who would coach their students in the art of speech-making. They charged very high fees for this. Socrates in contrast didn't charge for his services. In fact he claimed he didn't know anything, so how could he teach at all? This didn't stop students coming to him and listening in on his conversations. It didn't make him popular with the Sophists either.

7   One day his friend Chaerophon[5] went to the Oracle of Apollo at Delphi[6]. The oracle was a wise old woman, a sibyl, who would answer questions that visitors asked. Her answers were usually in the form of a riddle. "Is anyone wiser than Socrates?" Chaerophon asked. "No," came the answer. "No one is wiser than Socrates."

8   When Chaerophon told Socrates about this he didn't believe it at first. It really puzzled him. "How can I be the wisest man in Athens when I know so little?" he wondered. He devoted years to questioning people to see if anyone was wiser than he was. Finally he realized what the oracle had meant and that she had been right. Lots of people were good at the various things they did—carpenters were good at carpentry, and soldiers knew about fighting. But none of them were truly wise. They didn't really know what they were talking about.

9   The word "philosopher" comes from the Greek words meaning "love of wisdom". The Western tradition in philosophy spread from ancient Greece across large parts of the world, at time cross-fertilized by ideas from the East. The kind of wisdom that it values is based on argument, reasoning and asking questions, not on believing things simply because someone important has told you they are true. Wisdom for Socrates was not knowing lots of facts, or knowing how to do something. It meant understanding the true nature of our existence, including the limits of what we can know. Philosophers today are doing more or less what Socrates was doing: asking tough questions, looking at reasons and evidence, struggling to answer some of the most important questions we can ask ourselves about the nature of reality and how we should live.

10   What made Socrates so wise was that he kept asking questions and he was always willing to debate his ideas. Life, he declared, is only worth living if you think about what you are doing. An unexamined existence is all right for cattle, but not for human beings.

11   Unusually for a philosopher, Socrates refused to write anything down. For him talking was far better than writing. Written words can't answer back; they explain anything to you when you don't understand them. Face-to-face conversation was much better, he maintained. In conversation we can take into account the kind of person we are talking to; we can adapt what we say so that the message gets across. Because he refused to write, it's mainly through the work of Socrates' star pupil Plato[7] that we have much idea of what this great man believed and argued about. Plato wrote down a series of conversations between Socrates and the people he questioned. These are known as the *Platonic Dialogues* and are great works of literature as

well as of philosophy—in some ways Plato was the Shakespeare of his day. Reading these dialogues, we get a sense of what Socrates was like, how clever he was and how infuriating.

12 Athens as a whole didn't value Socrates. Far from it. Many Athenians felt that Socrates was dangerous and was deliberately undermining the government. In 399 BC, when Socrates was 70 years old, one of them, Meletus[8], took him to court. He claimed that Socrates was neglecting the Athenian gods, introducing new gods of his own. He also suggested that Socrates was teaching the young men of Athens to behave badly, encouraging them to turn against the authorities. These were both very serious accusations. It is difficult to know now how accurate they were. Perhaps Socrates really did discourage his students from following the state religion, and there is some evidence that he enjoyed mocking Athenian democracy. That would have been consistent with his character. What is certainly true is that many Athenians believed the charges.

The Death of Socrates, by Jacques-Louis David in 1787

13 They voted on whether or not he was guilty. Just over half of the 501 citizens who made up the huge jury thought he was, and sentenced him to death. If he'd wanted to, he could probably have talked his way out of being executed. But instead, true to his reputation as a gadfly, he annoyed the Athenians even more by arguing that he had done nothing wrong and that they should, in fact, be rewarding him by giving him free meals for life instead of punishing him. That didn't go down well.

14 He was put to death by being forced to drink poison made from hemlock, a plant that gradually paralyses the body. Socrates said goodbye to his wife and three sons, and then gathered his students around him. If he had the choice to carry on living quietly, not asking any more difficult questions, he would not take it. He'd rather die than that. He had an inner voice that told him to keep questioning everything, and he could not betray it. Then he drank the cup of poison. Very soon he was dead.

15 In Plato's dialogues, though, Socrates lives on. This difficult man, who kept asking questions and would rather die than stop thinking about how things really are, has been an inspiration for philosophers ever since.

(Source: *A Little History of Philosophy* by Nigel Warburton, reprint edition, October 30, 2012.)

Notes

1. **Nigel Warburton** is a British philosopher, writer, and podcaster. Warburton has also authored *Philosophy: The Basics*, a popular introductory text used in many philosophy courses.

2. **The Peloponnesian War** (431—404 BC) was a conflict fought between Athens and Sparta, along with their respective allies. It is named after the Peloponnese, the peninsula in southern Greece where Sparta was located. The Peloponnesian War had a profound impact on ancient Greece. It weakened the major Greek city-states and left them vulnerable to invasion from external forces. The war also demonstrated the limitations of democratic rule and led to a sense of disillusionment among Greeks regarding their political systems.

3. **Euthydemus** was a fleet commander for Athens during the Sicilian Expedition, 415 to 413 BC.

4. The **Sophists** were a group of ancient Greek philosophers who were active during the 5th and 4th centuries BC. They were known for their skills in rhetoric, oratory, and argumentation. The term "Sophist" comes from the Greek word "sophistes", which means "wise man" or "expert".

5. **Chaerophon** was a citizen of ancient Greece and friend of Socrates. He is primarily known for his association with Socrates and his role in seeking the Oracle of Delphi's opinion on Socrates' wisdom.

6. **The Oracle of Apollo** or the Oracle of Delphi was a priestess named Pythia, who supposedly delivered prophecies and advice from the god Apollo. People from all over Greece and beyond would visit Delphi to consult the oracle on various matters, including important decisions, political affairs, and personal issues. Delphi was an important religious and cultural center located on the slopes of Mount Parnassus in central Ancient Greece. The city of Delphi was primarily known for the Oracle of Delphi, which was believed to be the most prestigious oracle in ancient Greece.

7. **Plato** (428—348 BC), an ancient Greek philosopher, is widely recognized as one of the most significant figures in Western philosophy. A student of Socrates, Plato went on to become the teacher of Aristotle, forming an influential lineage of philosophical thought. His philosophical works, written in the form of dialogues, explore a wide range of topics, including ethics, politics, metaphysics, epistemology, and the nature of reality.

8. **Meletus** was a tragic poet in ancient Greece, known for his prosecuting role in the trial and eventual execution of the philosopher Socrates.

Remembering and Understanding

Activity 1 True or False Questions

Are the following statements true or false? Make your decisions based on the text.

(　) 1. Socrates was not only wise and brave but physically attractive and well-groomed.

Extensive Reading 3

( ) 2. Socrates aimed to prove he was the wisest man when asking people those seemingly simple but actually razor-sharp questions.

( ) 3. Socrates was very rich because he charged high fees for his teaching services.

( ) 4. Socrates believed that wisdom lies in knowing many facts.

( ) 5. The oracle at Delphi declared that Socrates was the wisest man in Athens.

( ) 6. Socrates refused to write anything down because he believed face-to-face conversation was superior.

( ) 7. Socrates encouraged his students to follow the state religion of Athens.

( ) 8. Athenians valued and revered Socrates during his lifetime.

( ) 9. Socrates argued that he should be rewarded with free meals for life instead of being punished.

( ) 10. Socrates attempted to escape execution by pleading guilty.

( ) 11. Socrates was executed by drinking poison made from hemlock.

( ) 12. Socrates left behind a written body of work, detailing his own philosophical ideas.

( ) 13. Socrates' death had a lasting impact on the development of philosophy.

Activity 2 Identify and Synthesize Information

Socrates has been called "the man who asked questions". What can we learn about the characteristics of Socratic questioning? Fill out the blanks in the chart based on the information given in the text.

Characteristics	Further explanations
Challenging assumptions	Socrates questioned people's beliefs and assumptions, aiming to expose contradictions or (1)_____ in their thinking.
Refining concepts	He engaged in conversations to clarify and refine concepts, often using (2)_____ to highlight the (3)_____ of people's understanding.
Probing for Knowledge	Socrates sought to uncover knowledge by asking (4)_____ questions rather than asserting his own knowledge or answers.
Encouraging (5)_____	Through dialogue, Socrates led individuals to examine their own understanding and realize their (6)_____, pushing them to question and seek deeper insights.
Pursuit of (7)_____	Socrates believed that wisdom came from recognizing one's lack of (8)_____ and continually questioning, examining, and challenging ideas.
(9)_____ conversation	Socrates preferred oral dialogue over (10)_____ texts, emphasizing the importance of interactive communication to adapt to the interlocutor and facilitate understanding.

Unit 3 Learning to Ask Questions

 Reasoning and Analyzing

Answer the following questions.

1. What kind of impact did Socrates have on the field of philosophy?
   _____
   _____

2. Why was Socrates seen as an annoying and dangerous influence by some in Athens?
   _____
   _____

3. Why did Socrates believe that being deceitful could be moral in certain situations?
   _____
   _____

4. What did the Oracle of Apollo at Delphi mean when she declared Socrates to be the wisest man in Athens?
   _____
   _____

5. How did Socrates define wisdom?
   _____
   _____

6. Why did Socrates refuse to write anything down?
   _____
   _____

7. Why did Socrates argue that he should be rewarded with free meals for life instead of being punished?
   _____
   _____

8. Why did Socrates choose to drink hemlock and face execution instead of living quietly without asking difficult questions?
   _____
   _____

9. How did Plato's dialogues contribute to the preservation of Socrates' philosophy?
   _____
   _____

10. How did Socrates continue to inspire philosophers after his death?
    _____
    _____

Extensive Reading 3

 Reflecting and Creating

Activity 1 Topics for Discussion and Writing

1. "What made Socrates so wise was that he kept asking questions". Do you agree with the idea that questioning is essential in the pursuit of knowledge and wisdom? Why or why not? Can you think of any potential limitations or drawbacks to Socrates' emphasis on questioning? Have a discussion in your group and support your arguments with examples and evidence from the text, as well as any external knowledge or personal experiences.

2. Socrates is considered the patron saint of philosophy, and his influence greatly shaped the subject. Write a paragraph evaluating the impact of Socrates on the field of philosophy. Use evidence from the text or other sources to support your evaluation. Consider both the positive and negative aspects of Socrates' influence.

3. Choose a Chinese philosopher who you are familiar with. Imagine a dialogue between Socrates and the Chinese philosopher, focusing on a specific philosophical topic or question. Write the dialogue, incorporating Socratic questioning techniques and the views of the Chinese philosopher.

Activity 2 Debate: Is Face-to-Face Communication Superior to Writing?

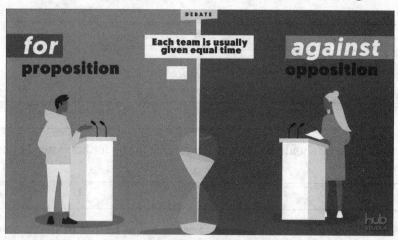

Debating Skills—Introduction. Source: Hub Scuola

Socrates believed that face-to-face communication was superior to writing. However, in today's digital age, where written communication is prevalent through various media, can we still argue that face-to-face communication holds the same level of superiority? In what ways might written communication offer unique advantages or benefits that surpass or complement face-to-face interaction? Get into two groups and engage in a debate to critically evaluate and argue for or against the idea that face-to-face communication is superior to writing.

Text B The Symposium (Excerpt)

Preparatory Work

Activity 1 Brainstorming: Word Association

Here are some key terms from Plato's dialogue The Symposium: "love" "beauty" "tenderness" "desire" and "goodness". Brainstorm associations, thoughts, or emotions related to each word and how these words are interconnected. Make connections to your prior knowledge or personal experiences. Share and discuss your ideas as a class.

Source: Course Hero

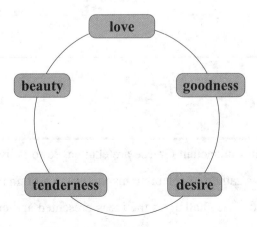

Extensive Reading 3

Activity 2 Learn About the Main Characters in *The Symposium*

(Oil painting: Plato's *Symposium*, by Anselm Feuerbach)

The text is excerpted from *The Symposium*, a philosophical dialogue written by Plato. *The Symposium* records some speeches on Love given by a group of notable men in Athens. Here is a list of the seven speakers at the symposium; please find some background information about them and complete the table.

Speaker	What I know about him
Phaedrus	
Pausanias	
Eryximachus	
Aristophanes	
Agathon	
Socrates	
Alcibiades	

Reading the Text

> What is love? Several elites in ancient Greece are challenged to deliver a speech in turn in praise of Love at the banquet hosted by Agathon to celebrate his victory in a drama festival. Socrates is among the invited guests. At the symposium, he challenges the ideas presented and employs a series of questions to explore the essence of Love.

The Symposium[1] (Excerpt)

Plato

Agathon:

1   I wish first to explain how my speech should proceed, and then to proceed with my speech. All the earlier speakers seem to me not to have been eulogising the god but felicitating humans on the good things of which he is the source. But no one has described the nature of him who has bestowed these good things. Since the only proper way to make a eulogy of anyone is to describe first his nature and then the nature of the good things of which he is the source, so in the case of Love[2] it is right for us to praise first his nature and then his gifts.

2   Now, it is my contention that of those happy beings, the gods, the happiest of all—if they will allow me to say so without taking offence—is Love, because he is supreme in beauty and goodness. He is the most beautiful in the following ways. First, he is the youngest of the gods, and he himself provides good evidence for what I say, for by his speed he outstrips old age, and everyone knows how fast old age advances; at any rate it comes upon us faster than it should. Love has a natural hatred of old age and never approaches anywhere near it. He always consorts with the young—"like goes with like", the old saying is right—so he is young himself.

3   So, Love is young, and as well as being young he is tender. But he lacks a poet like Homer[3] who can demonstrate his tenderness, as Homer does for Ate[4] when he says that she is both a goddess and tender—or her feet at least are tender.

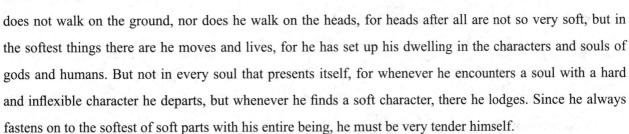

> "Tender are her feet, for not on the ground does she set them,
> But stepping on the heads of men she makes her way."

4   He seems to me to give clear evidence of her tenderness when he says that she does not walk on what is hard but only on what is soft, and we will use the same sort of evidence to show that Love too is tender. For Love does not walk on the ground, nor does he walk on the heads, for heads after all are not so very soft, but in the softest things there are he moves and lives, for he has set up his dwelling in the characters and souls of gods and humans. But not in every soul that presents itself, for whenever he encounters a soul with a hard and inflexible character he departs, but whenever he finds a soft character, there he lodges. Since he always fastens on to the softest of soft parts with his entire being, he must be very tender himself.

5   So, then, he is very young and very tender, and he is supple in form as well. For if he were hard and inflexible he would not be able to enfold his object completely nor to pass unnoticed through the entire soul as he enters and leaves. Good evidence of his lithe and supple form is his gracefulness, which all agree Love

possesses to an exceptional degree. For gracelessness and Love are always at war. Love spends his time among flowers: that is the reason for the beauty of his complexion. But where there is no bloom of body or soul or of anything else, or where the bloom has withered, there Love does not alight; but where there is a place full of flowers and fragrance, there he settles and remains.

Socrates:

6   It was then I realised what a fool I had been in agreeing with you to take my turn and deliver a eulogy of Love, and in saying I was an expert on the subject of love, despite, as it turned out, knowing nothing about how to compose a eulogy of anything. For in my naivety I thought I had only to speak the truth about the subject of the eulogy. This should be the foundation, I thought, and on the basis of the facts one selected the finest examples and arranged them to best effect. Assuming, then, that I knew the true way to eulogise, I even felt confident that I was going to speak well. But actually, as it now appears, this is not the way to deliver a eulogy at all. Instead one should attribute to the subject the greatest and finest qualities possible whether they are truly there or not, and if what one says is not true, that doesn't matter.

7   I certainly thought you began your speech in the right way, my dear Agathon, when you said you had first to demonstrate what kind of being Love is, and then to proceed to his characteristic activity. That is the sort of beginning I very much approve of. And since you have already described in magnificent style what he is like, please tell me this further thing: is Love such that he is love of something, or is he love of nothing? Suppose I asked you about the essential meaning of the word "father", and whether "father" was a father of something or not. To give the right answer you would surely reply that "father" was a father of a son or of a daughter.

8   'Isn't that so?'

9   'Of course,' said Agathon.

10   'And you would say the same in the case of a mother?' Agathon agreed.

11   'Then perhaps you wouldn't object to answering a few more questions,' said Socrates, 'so that you will understand better what I have in mind. If I were to ask you, "What about the essential meaning of 'brother': is 'brother' a brother of something or is he not?" ' Agathon said he was.

12   'Of a brother or a sister?'

13   'Yes.'

14   'Now,' said Socrates. 'apply the same test to love. Is Love love of something or is he love of nothing?'

15   'Certainly Love is love of something.'

16   'Well then, keep this in your mind, remembering what it is that Love is love of,' said Socrates, 'and for now tell me this: does Love desire that thing which he is love of, or not?'

17   'Certainly he desires it.'

18 'And does he desire and love it when he has in his possession that thing which he desires and loves, or when he does not have it?'

19 'Probably when he does not have it,' said Agathon.

20 'Now, instead of saying "probably",' said Socrates, 'consider whether it isn't necessarily true that that which desires, desires what it lacks, or, put another way, there is no desire if there is no lack. That seems to me, Agathon, an inescapable conclusion. What do you think?'

21 'It seems so to me too.'

22 'Very good. So, would a man who was tall wish to be tall, or a man who was strong wish to be strong?'

23 'From what has just been agreed that is impossible.'

24 'Exactly, because someone who has these attributes would not be lacking in them.'

25 'True.'

26 'But suppose,' said Socrates, 'that a man who was already strong also wished to be strong, or a fast runner also wished to be fast, or a healthy man healthy: in these and all similar cases you might perhaps imagine that people who are like this and have these particular attributes also desire to have the attributes they have (and I am saying all this because I don't want us to get the wrong idea). If you think about it, Agathon, it must be the case that these people already possess their respective attributes whether they want to or not, and why would they also desire to have what they have? Therefore, when someone says, "I am healthy and I wish to be healthy", or "I am rich and I wish to be rich", or, "I desire exactly what I have", we will say to him, "My friend, you already possess wealth (or health or strength). What you really wish for is the continuing possession of these things in the future, for at the moment you have them whether you wish it or not." When you say, "I desire what I already have," consider whether you don't actually mean, "I wish I may continue to have in the future what I already have at present." Surely our friend would agree?'

27 Agathon assented.

28 Socrates went on, 'So, then, he desires the possession and presence in the future of those things which he has at present. But isn't this equivalent to loving that thing which is not yet available to him and which he does not yet have?'

29 'Certainly it is.'

30 'Then this man and everyone who feels desire, desires what is not in his possession or presence, so that what he does not have, or what he is not, or what he lacks, these are the sorts of things that are the objects of desire and love. Isn't

Source: BBC Radio 4—In Our Time, Plato's *Symposium*

Extensive Reading 3

this so?'

31 'Certainly.'

32 'Well now,' said Socrates, 'let us sum up our conclusions so far. Isn't Love, first, of something, and, secondly, of something that he lacks?'

33 'Yes.'

34 'On this basis, then, please recall what you said in your speech that Love was love of. I will remind you if you like. I think you said something like this, that the interests of the gods were established by reason of their love of beautiful things; for there is no love of ugly things, you said. Didn't you say something like this?'

35 'Yes I did.'

36 'And reasonably enough, Agathon,' said Socrates. 'And if this is the case, then surely Love is love of beauty and not of ugliness?'

37 Agathon agreed.

38 'And we have already agreed that what he loves is what he lacks and does not possess?'

39 'Yes.'

40 'Then the conclusion is that what Love lacks and does not have is beauty.'

41 'That must be true.'

42 'And do you call a thing beautiful which lacks beauty and does not possess it in any respect?'

43 'Certainly not.'

44 'Then if this is so do you still say that Love is beautiful?'

45 To this Agathon replied, 'Socrates, it rather looks as though I understood nothing of what I was saying at the time.'

46 'You spoke very well, Agathon. Just one more small thing—doesn't what is good also seem to you beautiful?'

47 'Yes.'

48 'So if Love is lacking in what is beautiful, and what is good is beautiful, then he will also be lacking in what is good.'

49 'Socrates, I cannot argue against you, so let it be as you say.'

50 'There is no difficulty in arguing against Socrates, beloved Agathon; what you cannot argue against is the truth.'

(Source: *The Symposium*, reissue edition, April 29, 2003.)

Unit 3 Learning to Ask Questions

Notes

1. Excerpted from ***The Symposium***, the text is mainly about Agathon's eulogy of Love and Socrates' questioning against Agathon's understanding of the nature of Love. In ancient Greece, a symposium was a social gathering or banquet where men would come together to engage in intellectual discussions, drink wine, and enjoy entertainment. The word "symposium" comes from the Greek words "syn" (meaning "together") and "posis" (meaning "drinking"), reflecting the central role of drinking wine in these gatherings.

2. In Plato's *The Symposium*, the term "**Love**" typically refers to the concept of Eros, the Greek god of Love, which is a complex and multifaceted representation of love that goes beyond mere physical attraction or romantic affection. In the context of the dialogue, the participants, including Socrates, engage in a philosophical discussion about the nature of love and its various forms.

3. **Homer** is considered one of the greatest poets of ancient Greece and the author of two epic poems, the *Iliad* and the *Odyssey*. His works have had a profound influence on Western literature and culture.

4. **Ate** is, in Greek mythology, the personification of ruin, folly, and delusion (goddess).

Remembering and Understanding

Activity 1 Summarize Agathon's Eulogy

The first section of the text is part of Agathon's eulogy on Love. Fill in the blanks with appropriate words to get a brief summary of it.

Agathon's Eulogy on Love

Agathon argues that Love is the happiest among the gods due to his (1)_____. Firstly, he describes Love as (2)_____, constantly (3)_____ old age and always (4)_____ the young. Then Love is portrayed as (5)_____, much like Ate in Homer's writings, as he moves and resides within the (6)_____ of gods and humans. Finally, Agathon emphasizes Love's (7)_____, evident in his graceful and delicate nature. Love thrives where there is fragrance and beauty, avoiding places where (8)_____.

Activity 2 Summarize the Dialogue Between Socrates and Agathon

Socrates' questions	Agathon's responses
1. Is Love such that he is love of something, or is he love of nothing?	
2.	

Extensive Reading 3

(continued)

3.	
4.	
5.	
6.	
7.	
8.	
9.	

Reasoning and Analyzing

Activity 1 Multiple-choice Questions

Choose the best answer from the four choices given based on the text.

1. In Agathon's speech, what is his primary contention about? .

   A. Love is the youngest of the gods.

   B. Love is the fastest of the gods.

   C. Love is the most beautiful of the gods.

   D. Love provides evidence of his tenderness.

2. What does Socrates realize during Agathon's speech?

   A. He was wrong to volunteer for a eulogy on Love.

   B. Agathon has a deep understanding of Love.

   C. He is an expert in composing eulogies.

   D. Agathon's speech is based on truth and substance.

3. How does Socrates criticize Agathon's approach to delivering a eulogy?

   A. Agathon did not praise Love's gifts enough.

   B. Agathon did not describe Love's nature accurately.

   C. Agathon did not attribute the greatest qualities possible to Love.

76

D. Agathon mentioned irrelevant details about Love.

4. Socrates argues that someone who already possesses certain attributes would not desire them because _____.

   A. desire only arises from a sense of lack

   B. possession of attributes eliminates the desire

   C. people are incapable of desiring what they already have

   D. attributes lose their value once they are possessed

5. How does Socrates argue that Love desires what he lacks?

   A. Love is incapable of possessing anything.

   B. Love desires things that are unattainable.

   C. Love is constantly changing and evolving.

   D. Love desires the future possession of things in his present state.

6. Why does Agathon concede that Love may be lacking in what is good?

   A. Because Socrates presents compelling evidence.

   B. Because he cannot argue against Socrates' reasoning.

   C. Because he realizes the flaw in his earlier argument.

   D. Because Love's nature is inherently flawed.

7. How does Agathon respond to Socrates' argument?

   A. He agrees with Socrates.

   B. He refuses to argue.

   C. He argues against Socrates.

   D. He questions Socrates' reasoning.

8. Based on the final statement, Socrates believes his argument _____.

   A. is difficult to refute

   B. is open to interpretation

   C. lacks substance and truth

   D. is a reflection of his pursuit of wisdom

▶ Reflecting and Creating

Activity 1 Topics for Discussion and Writing

1. In his eulogy on Love, Agathon argues Love is the happiest among the gods due to his supreme beauty and goodness, which is supported by three specific arguments. Do you think Agathon's arguments are acceptable and reasonable? Is his speech genuine praise or flattery? Evaluate the validity and strength of

Extensive Reading 3

these arguments, supporting your analysis and evaluation with evidence from the text, and exchange your views in groups.

2. In response to Agathon's eulogy, Socrates engages Agathon in a dialogue, challenging him with a series of questions and pointing out the flaws and inconsistencies in his speech. Socrates argues that Love cannot possess beauty since Love itself desires beauty. Do you think Love desires a thing which he is love of and what he lacks? Write a short essay discussing the relationship between love, desire, and beauty. You can refer to the text, your personal experiences, or prior knowledge.

Activity 2 Role-play

Get into groups of five. Each quintuple should create a dialogue between a teacher (played by one of the group members) and a group of four students, focusing on a topic or question and incorporating Socratic questioning techniques. Present the dialogue in class.

Topic: Any philosophical question or hot topic that intrigues you, such as love, justice, climate change, online privacy, or data security.

Role 1: Teacher
Role 2~5: Student A, B, C, D

Summary

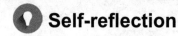

Self-reflection

Fill out the checklist.

Area	Yes / No?	Notes / Comment
I know the essence of Socratic questioning.		
I know the significance of Socratic questioning in critical reading and critical thinking.		
I know the different categories of Socratic questions.		
I know how to ask questions like Socrates to cultivate critical thinking.		
I now have a deeper understanding of Love.		

Unit 3 Learning to Ask Questions

 Value Cultivation

Translate the following quotes either in English or Chinese and explain them in your own words.

1. 仁爱之心至于无物则落，至于有物则成。——（东汉）王充《论衡》

2. 君子学必好问，问与学，相辅而行者也，非学无以致疑，非问无以广识。

——（清）刘开《孟涂文集》

3. 教育是一门"仁而爱人"的事业，爱是教育的灵魂，没有爱就没有教育。

——习近平同北京师范大学师生代表座谈时的讲话

4. Love is a desire for self-immortalization and for perpetual possession of the Good and Beautiful.

—Socrates

5. The one real goal of education is to leave a person asking questions.

—Max Beerbohm

6. The important thing is not to stop questioning. Curiosity has its own reason for existing.

—Albert Einstein

 Further Reading

1. 习近平同北京师范大学师生代表座谈时的讲话（2014年9月9日）

2. The Thinker's Guide to the Art of Socratic Questioning by Richard Paul and Linda Elder (2016)

3. *The Symposium* by Plato (English version, 1795)

Value Cultivation

Translate the following quotes either in English or in Chinese and explain them in your own words:

1. 十五志于学，三十而立，四十不惑，五十知天命，……——（孔子，《论语·为政》）

2. 千里之行，始于足下。知耻近乎勇，知耻而后勇，非勇之以耻。
   ——《礼记·中庸》

3. 学而不厌，诲人不倦。……知之者不如好之者，好之者不如乐之者。
   ——孔子《论语·述而》《论语·雍也》

4. Love is a desire for self-immortalization and for perpetual possession of the Good and Beautiful.
   ——Socrates

5. The one real goal of education is to leave a person asking questions.
   ——Max Beerbohm

6. The important thing is not to stop questioning. Curiosity has its own reason for existing.
   ——Albert Einstein

Further Reading

1. 刘儒德 主编：《教育心理学》，高等教育出版社，2010 年第 2 版.
2. The Thinker's Guide to the Art of Socratic Questioning by Richard Paul and Linda Elder, 2016.
3. The Symposium by Plato (English version, 385).

Unit 4
Understanding Arguments: The Basics

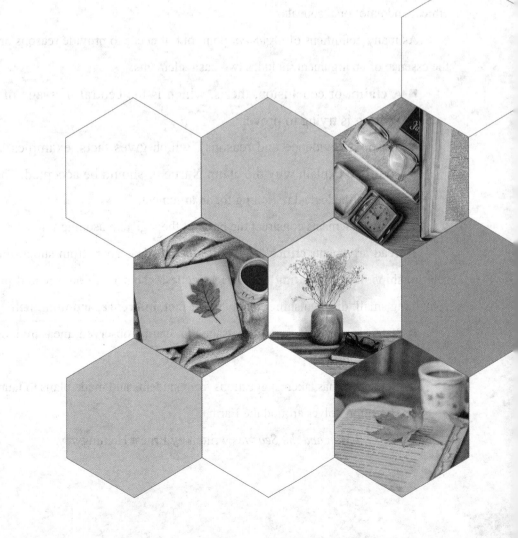

Extensive Reading 3

Mastering Critical Reading

Critical reading relates closely with arguments, whose purpose, usually, is to prove an assertion so the audience accepts it. The word *argument* may remind you of a quarrel, conflict, and heated debate. It is true that disagreements and disputes prevail everywhere due to the different natures, interests, and standpoints among people, but such confrontation from disagreement cannot cover the entire meaning of *argument*.

In logic and philosophy, an **argument** is a series of statements typically used to persuade someone of something or to present reasons for accepting a conclusion. Other definitions would point to a statement or statements providing support for a proposition. An argument, according to most authorities, gives primary importance to logical appeals. Yet, real-life arguments, especially on some controversial issues, also employ ethical and emotional appeals in order to convince, or rather, persuade, readers since we can always be influenced through various means, rational and nonrational alike, though to different extents. Thus, the arguments discussed here include those writings which rely heavily on logical reasoning, and also those with ethical and emotional appeals.

As many definitions of *argument* point out, it needs to provide reasons or evidence for a proposition, so the essence of an argument includes two basic elements:

- **A claim**, or conclusion, thesis, which is the central message of the writing and is what the writing is trying to prove.
- **Support** (evidence and reasons), which gives facts, examples, authoritative testimony, and so on, to explain why the claim is true or should be accepted. These two elements construct the basis of the logical reasoning for an argument.

These two elements construct the basis of the logical reasoning for an argument.

To read arguments critically involves taking ideas apart from supporting evidence, figuring out their relationships, and evaluating their effectiveness. That is a complicated process, but we can start with something small: distinguishing statements of **fact, inference,** and **judgment**.

- Statements of **fact** carry a message that can be observed, measured, or confirmed. Facts are open to verification.
  - ❖ Our school has taken suggestions from students and made plans to launch a number of programs.
  - ❖ The sun revolves around the Earth.
  - ❖ *The Old Man and the Sea* was written by Ernest Hemingway.

Unit 4 Understanding Arguments: The Basics

 Which of the example statements above is false to people nowadays? Do you think it is a statement of fact?

Facts are verifiable, which means we can check them against our observations or trusted sources. In our discussion, factual statements go beyond the conventional concept of facts, encompassing events known to have occurred or circumstances known to have existed, as well as those verified as false. Furthermore, the truthfulness of a "fact" can evolve as our understanding of the world grows.

■ **Inferences** are statements about the unknown based on our analysis of the known. In other words, they are figured out from what we observe or can confirm. However, because what we know and how we interpret messages may vary greatly, the conclusions we draw can be very different. In this sense, inferences exist within the individual.

To evaluate a statement of inference, we can verify the facts involved and examine the connection drawn between them. Based on the result of our evaluation, we may agree or disagree with the inference, but again, our acceptance would not change its being an inference.

❖ Smoking is a serious health hazard.
❖ Mr. Johnson is a punctual person regarding his appointments.
❖ Dogs are more popular pets than cats in this city.

? How would you evaluate the example inference above about the popularity of dogs and cats as pets? What facts are needed in this case? What is the connection assumed between the facts and the conclusion? Is the assumption acceptable to you?

■ **Judgments** are opinions that imply approval or disapproval of persons, objects, situations, and actions. That means that judgments are personal opinions and subjective, based on our values, beliefs, or tastes. A judgment may also be embedded in compulsion with words like "should" or "must". To evaluate statements of judgment, we need to identify the facts and inferences involved, verify the facts, assess whether the inferences are adequately justified, and decide whether the values or beliefs assumed are acceptable.

Though judgments are subjective and often reflect our values, beliefs, or tastes, which may vary greatly from person to person, that doesn't mean we can't, or shouldn't, argue about them. Trying to persuade others to see our point of view or accept our values is an important part of communication and life. On the other hand, listening to other people explain or reason for their values or beliefs helps us examine our own, and that's also the point of being open-minded.

❖ Anhui cuisine is the most delicious.
❖ Smoking should be prohibited in all public places.

83

Extensive Reading 3

❖ Animal experiments are cruel.

> **?** Distinguish the example above about smoking with these statements:
> a) Smoking causes more than 1 million deaths in our country each year.
> b) According to the data available, smoking has become a fatal health hazard.
> What kind of statements are they, respectively?

Based on our understanding of the differences between statements of fact, inference, and judgment, we can expect certain characteristics of arguments.

■ **Arguments start from an arguable issue.**

To make a meaningful argument, we usually don't argue about hard facts, like "The sun rises in the east," or "Our school year usually starts on September 1". These facts are easily checked and there is no need to argue about them. Similarly, we seldom argue about subjective opinions, like our personal preferences. Whether you like chocolate ice cream more than strawberry ice cream may only be explained from your personal tastes. Such opinions will not lead to a meaningful argument.

■ **Arguments rest on facts and inference for evidence and reasons.**

Just stating our ideas is far from building an argument. Besides giving a proposition, more importantly, we need to present sufficient and relevant support to prove it, thereby leading the audience to accept it naturally. Similarly, to analyze arguments, we need to be especially careful in locating the supporting facts and justifiable inferences in order to decide how we should react to the argument.

■ **Arguments usually have embedded values.**

Any argument should be based on evidence and reasons, but it also often incorporates values, explicit or implicit. When trying to prove their claims, writers will inevitably give their beliefs or base their reasoning on the assumptions of values that they suppose the audience will share. Some values may be genuinely common among most people, like integrity, honesty, and diligence, while others may be specific to some cultures, like individuality. Thus, analyzing arguments calls especially for critical reading.

A study in argument offers many invaluable benefits. Because people are so inclined to approve of arguments that are consistent with their own opinions and dismiss those that are not, the knowledge of argumentation will equip us with the ability to stay sensible in the bewildering confusion of voices around us, evaluate the validity of claims, and decide whether to accept them. Also, a critical and sensible reader can distinguish good arguments from bad ones, though we may not necessarily agree with the claims.

Unit 4 Understanding Arguments: The Basics

Text A Your Brain Lies to You

 Preparatory Work

Activity 1 Experience Sharing

Think of your experiences of being cheated by your brain, eyes, or ears. For example, have you ever had any illusion of having already experienced a certain situation when you actually have not, a feeling called déjà vu? Share your experience in class. How did you feel at that time? Frightened? Excited? Bewildered? Any other feelings? How would you explain those experiences?

My experience/ my classmate's experience	My feeling	My explanation

Activity 2 Groundless Beliefs

Sometimes, we hold tight to ideas even though we cannot remember where they came from or we know we have no sound evidence to back them up. These beliefs, with no solid support, are called groundless beliefs. What such beliefs do you have? Why do people believe in such ideas?

My groundless beliefs	
Possible causes	

Extensive Reading 3

Reading the Text

> In the text, the authors propose that our brains do not naturally obey the assumption that "ideas are more likely to spread if they are honest"; instead, they lie to us. How does this organ, as the controller of our body, lie to us? How can we protect ourselves against the deception?

Your Brain Lies to You

Sam Wang & Sandra Aamodt[1]

1 False beliefs are everywhere. Eighteen percent of Americans think the sun revolves around the earth, one poll has found. Thus it seems slightly less egregious that, according to another poll, 10 percent of us think that Senator Barack Obama, a Christian, is instead a Muslim. The Obama campaign has created a Web site to dispel misinformation. But this effort may be more difficult than it seems, thanks to the quirky way in which our brains store memories—and mislead us along the way.

2 The brain does not simply gather and stockpile information as a computer's hard drive does. Current research suggests that facts may be stored first in the hippocampus, a structure deep in the brain about the size and shape of a fat man's curled pinkie finger. But the information does not rest there. Every time we recall it, our brain writes it down again, and during this re-storage, it is also reprocessed. In time, the fact is gradually transferred to the cerebral cortex and is separated from the context in which it was originally learned. For example, you know that the capital of California is Sacramento, but you probably don't remember how you learned it.

3 This phenomenon, known as source amnesia, can also lead people to forget whether a statement is true. Even when a lie is presented with a disclaimer, people often later remember it as true.

4 With time, this misremembering only gets worse. A false statement from a non-credible source that is at first not believed can gain credibility during the months it takes to reprocess memories from short-term hippocampal storage to longer-term cortical storage. As the source is forgotten, the message and its implications gain strength. This could explain why, during the 2004 presidential campaign, it took some weeks for the Swift Boat Veterans for Truth campaign against Senator John Kerry[2] to have an effect on his standing in the polls.

5 Even if they do not understand the neuroscience behind source amnesia, campaign strategists can exploit it to spread misinformation. They know that if their message is initially memorable, its impression will persist long after it is debunked. In repeating a falsehood, someone may back it up with an opening line like "I think I read somewhere" or even with a reference to a specific source.

6 In one study, a group of Stanford students was exposed repeatedly to an unsubstantiated claim taken

from a Web site that Coca-Cola is an effective paint thinner. Students who read the statement five times were nearly one-third more likely than those who read it only twice to attribute it to *Consumer Reports* (rather than *The National Enquirer*, their other choice), giving it a gloss of credibility.

7   Adding to this innate tendency to mold information we recall is the way our brains fit facts into established mental frameworks. We tend to remember news that accords with our worldview, and discount statements that contradict it.

8   In another Stanford study, 48 students, half of whom said they favored capital punishment and half of whom said they opposed it, were presented with two pieces of evidence, one supporting and one contradicting the claim that capital punishment deters crime. Both groups were more convinced by the evidence that supported their initial position.

Source: http://www.soutu123.com/png/362051.html

9   Psychologists have suggested that legends propagate by striking an emotional chord. In the same way, ideas can spread by emotional selection, rather than by their factual merits, encouraging the persistence of falsehoods about Coke—or about a presidential candidate.

10   Journalists and campaign workers may think they are acting to counter misinformation by pointing out that it is not true. But by repeating a false rumor, they may inadvertently make it stronger. In its concerted effort to "stop the smears", the Obama campaign may want to keep this in mind. Rather than emphasize that Mr. Obama is not a Muslim, for instance, it may be more effective to stress that he embraced Christianity as a young man.

11   Consumers of news, for their part, are prone to selectively accept and remember statements that reinforce beliefs they already hold. In a replication of the study of students' impressions of evidence about the death penalty, researchers found that even when subjects were given a specific instruction to be objective, they were still inclined to reject evidence that disagreed with their beliefs.

12   In the same study, however, when subjects were asked to imagine their reaction if the evidence had pointed to the opposite conclusion, they were more open-minded to information that contradicted their beliefs. Apparently, it pays for consumers of controversial news to take a moment and consider that the opposite interpretation may be true.

13   In 1919, Justice Oliver Wendell Holmes of the Supreme Court[3] wrote that "the best test of truth is the power of the thought to get itself accepted in the competition of the market". Holmes erroneously assumed that ideas are more likely to spread if they are honest. Our brains do not naturally obey this admirable dictum, but by better understanding the mechanisms of memory perhaps we can move closer to Holmes's ideal.

(Source: nytimes.com, June 27, 2008.)

Extensive Reading 3

Notes

1. **Samuel S. H. Wang** is a professor of neuroscience at Princeton University, where he manages a research lab. **Sandra Aamodt**, former editor of *Nature Neuroscience*, is a neuroscientist and science writer. Drs. Wang and Aamodt are the authors of *Welcome to Your Brain: Why You Lose Your Car Keys but Never Forget How to Drive and Other Puzzles of Everyday Life* (2008) and *Welcome to Your Child's Brain: How the Mind Grows from Conception to College* (2011).

2. **Swift Boat Veterans for Truth**, rebranded as Swift Vets and POWs for Truth, was a political advocacy organization of United States Swift boat veterans and former prisoners of war of the Vietnam War, formed in the 2004 presidential election campaign against Democratic presidential nominee John Kerry.

3. **Oliver Wendell Holmes Jr.** (1841—1935) was an American jurist who served as a Supreme Court justice of the United States from 1902 to 1932.

 ## Remembering and Understanding

Activity 1 Draw a Diagram

In the text, the authors explain to us how our brains work in gathering and storing information. Draw a diagram to show this mechanism of memory in a lively way.

| |
| |
| |
| |
| |

According to the text, how do our brains "lie" to us?

_____

_____

Activity 2 Multiple-choice Questions

Choose the best answer from the four choices given based on the text.

1. What does the text mean by the first sentence, "False beliefs are everywhere"?

    A. False belief of the sun revolving around the Earth is held by too many people.

    B. False beliefs are common and ubiquitous.

    C. Barack Obama is actually a Christian, not a Muslim.

    D. False beliefs can be found in every corner of the world.

Unit 4 Understanding Arguments: The Basics

2. Which of the following is true about the hippocampus?

   A. It is a part of the brain that looks like a fat man's curled pinkie finger.

   B. It is a part of the brain that makes a fat man's finger curled and pinkie.

   C. It is a part of the brain that controls the size and shape of a man's fingers.

   D. It is a part of the brain that makes people with a curled pinkie finger grow fat.

3. What can source amnesia lead people to do?

   A. Fail to get the emotional chord of information.

   B. Forget the context in which information is learned.

   C. Restore information into the cerebral cortex easily.

   D. Distinguish true and false information easily.

4. According to the text, a better way to fight a rumor is to _____.

   A. point out directly that it is wrong

   B. give an emotional speech to reveal its falsehood

   C. stress the truth without repeating the wrong information often

   D. get it accepted in the competition of the market

5. What kind of information may be more easily accepted by people?

   A. Information that is emotional

   B. Information that contains truth only

   C. Information that is stored together with its context

   D. Information that agrees with people's established beliefs

Reasoning and Analyzing

Activity 1 Answer the Following Questions

1. What do the authors think of the effort by the Obama campaign to dispel misinformation? Why do they think that?

   _____
   _____

2. How is the human brain different from a computer hard drive?

   _____
   _____

3. Why did it take some weeks for the Swift Boat Veterans for Truth campaign against Senator John Kerry to have an effect on his standing in the polls? Can you make a guess about the general situation of that campaign?

Extensive Reading 3

4. What idea do the authors intend to support by mentioning the study about Coca-Cola in Para. 6? What may be the difference between *Consumer Reports* and *The National Enquirer* as implied in that paragraph?

_____

_____

5. What conclusion can you reach from the studies in Paras. 8, 11, and 12?

_____

_____

6. Why do the authors think that Justice Holmes made an "erroneous" statement?

_____

_____

7. Who do you think is the intended audience of this article? What clues from the article lead you to this conclusion?

_____

_____

8. What is the writing purpose of this article?

_____

_____

Activity 2 Distinguish Fact, Inference, and Judgment

Decide whether each of the following statements is Fact (F), Inference (I), or Judgment (J).

Statements	F	I	J
Eighteen percent of Americans think the sun revolves around the earth, one poll has found.			
It seems less egregious that many Americans think Barack Obama is a Muslim.			
The two authors hold that it seems less egregious that many Americans think Barack Obama is a Muslim.			
The human brain works in a more complicated way than a computer hard drive.			

Unit 4 Understanding Arguments: The Basics

(continued)

Campaign strategists will become more successful if they learn something about neuroscience.			
According to the studies from many researchers, people are very resistant to information opposite to their beliefs.			
It is dangerous to reveal the mechanisms of memory because they may be exploited by someone with an ill intention.			

 Reflecting and Creating

Activity 1 Topics for Discussion and Writing

1. In the text, the authors introduce briefly the working mechanism of the brain tackling information. In this sense, our brains "lie" to us. Looking into your own experience, have you ever suffered from "source amnesia"? Do you find you are more ready to accept information which matches your own beliefs? How harmful is this kind of belief?

2. According to the text, the way the brain works makes us prone to misinformation and narrow-mindedness. But is this biological factor the major reason for the situation that "false beliefs are everywhere"? What other factors can you think of? How do these factors contribute to the prevalence of false beliefs?

3. Since our brains are biologically set to "lie" to us, does it mean that we can do nothing to change the situation? After getting to know the mechanisms of memory, what do you think we can do to protect ourselves from being "cheated"?

Activity 2 Design a Campaign

Pick out a controversial topic recently or any issue of interest to you, and design a campaign to promote your proposal or candidate. List the procedures you are planning to use and give a scientific basis to back up each procedure.

Text B Why Doubt Is Essential to Science

 Preparatory Work

Activity 1 Speech from a Scientist

Have you ever dreamed of being a scientist? Which field of science are you interested in? What do you think

Extensive Reading 3

your life as a scientist would be like?

Suppose you are now a successful scientist and are invited to give a speech on your experiences to encourage young students. Exercise your imagination about this life and give your story. What urged you to be a scientist? What efforts have you made in realizing your dream? How important is your research now? What suggestions will you give to the young students? Design an outline to help with your speech. You can adapt the contents to be included in your speech.

Title of speech	
The beginning of my dream	
My efforts in realizing the dream	
Life as a scientist now	
Importance of my study	
My suggestions	
Other aspects (if any)	

Activity 2 Changing Life with Science and Technology

People often say that science and technology are changing life. Do you like these changes? Think of some of the most welcome changes science and technology have brought to your life. What changes are you expecting most in the future?

My opinion toward these changes	
Most welcome changes in my life	
Expected changes in the future	

Unit 4 Understanding Arguments: The Basics

Reading the Text

> For the public who are looking for certainties, why should they trust science, "a process that seems to require a troublesome state of uncertainty without always providing solid solutions"? How can we regain public trust in science when it is characterized by doubt?

Why Doubt Is Essential to Science

Liv Grjebine

1   The confidence people place in science is frequently based not on what it really is, but on what people would like it to be. When I asked students at the beginning of the year how they would define science, many of them replied that it is an objective way of discovering certainties about the world. But science cannot provide certainties. For example, a majority of Americans trust science as long as it does not challenge their existing beliefs. To the question "When science disagrees with the teachings of your religion, which one do you believe?", 58 percent of North Americans favor religion; 33 percent science; and 6 percent say "it depends".

2   But doubt in science is a feature, not a bug. Indeed, the paradox is that science, when properly functioning, questions accepted facts and yields both new knowledge and new questions—not certainty. Doubt does not create trust, nor does it help public understanding. So why should people trust a process that seems to require a troublesome state of uncertainty without always providing solid solutions?

Source: www.thepaper.cn/newsDetail_forward_13842985

3   As a historian of science, I would argue that it's the responsibility of scientists and historians of science to show that the real power of science lies precisely in what is often perceived as its weakness: its drive to question and challenge a hypothesis. Indeed, the scientific approach requires changing our understanding of

the natural world whenever new evidence emerges from either experimentation or observation. Scientific findings are hypotheses that encompass the state of knowledge at a given moment. In the long run, many are challenged and even overturned. Doubt might be troubling, but it impels us towards a better understanding; certainties, as reassuring as they may seem, in fact undermine the scientific process.

4   Scientists understand this, but in the dynamic between the public and science, there are two significant pitfalls.

5   The first is a form of blind scientism—that is, a belief in the capacity of science to solve all problems. The popular narrative of science is linear, embodied by heroic researchers who work selflessly for the good of humanity. Indeed, some scientists promote this attractive public image of their work. But this narrative ignores the ubiquity of controversy, conflict and error at the very heart of the scientific world. Such an idealized representation tends to turn science into an unquestionable set of beliefs. In fact, however, the power of science lies precisely in its capacity to generate discussion and even discord.

6   The second pitfall is a form of relativism borne out of a lack of confidence in the very existence of truth. It develops when science is divorced from method and viewed as just another claim in the marketplace of ideas. A Pew Research study shows that 35 percent of Americans think the scientific method can be used to produce "any result a researcher wants". Once the scientific approach has been delegitimized, then all hypotheses, including the most outlandish and irrational ones, can be taken as credible. So, hidden in this conceit of a democratic "marketplace of ideas" is a particularly virulent form of relativism that approaches nihilism.

7   Such examples of relativism about issues including climate change and, most recently, the COVID-19 pandemic—have significantly contributed to the proliferation of fake news and conspiracy theories. The diffusion of fake news is facilitated by the difficulty of a large majority of Americans in distinguishing between fact and opinion. Factual news can be proved or disproved by objective evidence, while opinion is an expression of the beliefs and values of the speaker.

8   In an effort to combat misinformation, scientists may overcompensate by accelerating their research, or publicizing their findings prematurely. This can spur dialogue about science but, with serious side effects. Some scientists have yielded to public pressure by rushing to provide theories about and potential cures for COVID-19. In an August article in the *Annals of Internal Medicine*[1], for example, Doroshow, et al. observe that "Although this boom has already begun to transform our response to the pandemic for the better, medical and scientific responses to past crises suggest that urgency may also result in compromised research quality and ethics, which may in turn jeopardize public faith in government and science, waste precious resources, and lead to the loss of human life".

9   The scientific process itself has been called into question during the pandemic in cases where the very

institutions and peer review process that were supposed to check scientific results failed to detect scams. In the words of editor Richard Horton, a study on hydroxychloroquine first published by *The Lancet*[2] and then retracted within weeks, was a "monumental fraud".

10   So how to regain public trust in science when the public is looking for certainties and when those who are supposed to impersonate doubt seem to be fickle or dogmatic?

Source: www.douban.com/note/686097549/?type=collect&_i=5655724rY1PTJw

11   A more realistic understanding of how science works can contribute to a better comprehension of the decisive role of doubt and skepticism in the scientific process. Indeed, science is not a linear path leading from one success to another, but rather a constant reevaluation of hypotheses. Failures are part of the scientific process and should be taught along with successes.

12   It is, therefore, not so much the content of scientific discoveries that should be highlighted, but the understanding of the scientific process itself that must be enhanced. No one expects the public at large to fully understand all discoveries or to be able to arbitrate between possible treatments. But what must be reaffirmed is that in science, doubt is not a vulnerability but a strength. The scientific approach often leads to dead ends, but sometimes it leads to fundamental discoveries that no other approach has ever achieved.

(Source: scientificamerican.com, October 9, 2020.)

Notes

1. ***Annals of Internal Medicine*** is the premier internal medicine journal established in 1927 by the American College of Physicians (ACP).
2. ***The Lancet***, a weekly peer-reviewed medical journal, is one of the world's oldest and best-known general medical journals, founded in 1823 by Thomas Wakley, an English surgeon. It has been owned by Elsevier since 1991.

Extensive Reading 3

✏️ Remembering and Understanding

Answer the following questions.

1. According to the author, what would people like science to be?

2. A paradox is a statement that contradicts itself and yet might be true (or false, at the same time). In Para. 2, the author refers to a "paradox". What is this paradox? What is the contradiction in this paradox?

3. According to the author, what is the real power of science? Who should shoulder the responsibility of showing people this power?

4. What is scientism? What is the popular narrative of science by scientism?

5. Where does relativism originate? And when does it develop? What's the problem with it?

6. What are the possible results of scientists' overcompensation efforts to combat misinformation?

7. What is the "more realistic understanding of how science works"(Para. 11)?

8. How important is doubt and skepticism in the scientific process?

Unit 4 Understanding Arguments: The Basics

Reasoning and Analyzing

Answer the following questions.

1. What point does the example in Para. 1 about science and religion illustrate?
   _____
   _____

2. What is your answer to the question at the end of Para. 2?
   _____
   _____

3. How can certainties undermine the scientific process as is proposed in Para. 3?
   _____
   _____

4. How is the popular narrative of science by scientism received among scientists? What is the author's attitude toward it? Why?
   _____
   _____

5. How can we explain the proliferation of fake news about COVID-19 with relativism? Are there any other reasons for the diffusion of fake news?
   _____
   _____

6. How serious is the mentioned retraction of the publication in *The Lancet*? Why?
   _____
   _____

7. Who does the author mean by "those who are supposed to impersonate doubt "(Para. 10)? Why are they supposed to impersonate doubt? In which sense do they seem to be fickle or dogmatic?
   _____
   _____

8. The author proposes that it is the understanding of the scientific process rather than the content of scientific discoveries that should be highlighted. Why?
   _____
   _____

Extensive Reading 3

Reflecting and Creating

Activity 1 Topics for Discussion and Writing

1. The author has given a way to distinguish fact and opinion in the article. "Factual news can be proved or disproved by objective evidence, while opinion is an expression of the beliefs and values of the speaker."(Para. 7) According to this principle, do you think the author's proposal that doubt is essential to science a fact or an opinion?

2. The author claims that doubt is essential to science. How does she support her claim? What kind of evidence does she use? How do you think of the effectiveness of this argument? Are you convinced? If yes, which reason or evidence do you think is most helpful in convincing you? If not, how can it be improved?

3. The author reminds us again and again in the article that science cannot provide certainties. Do you agree? If science cannot provide certainties, how does man know the world? If it provides certainties, what is wrong with the author's argument?

Activity 2 What Other Features?

In this writing, the author stresses the importance of doubt and skepticism. What other qualities or features do you think are also important to science? How do they compare to doubt? Pick out one feature that is more important than, or equally important to, or second to doubt. Think of some reasons to persuade your audience of the importance of this feature and note them down in the box.

The feature	
Reasons for its importance	

Summary

 ## Self-reflection

Fill out the checklist.

Area	Yes / No?	Notes / Comment
I know what argument and its basic elements are.		

Unit 4 Understanding Arguments: The Basics

(continued)

I know what statements of fact are.		
I know what statements of inference are.		
I know what statements of judgment are.		
I understand the characteristics of argument.		
I know how the brain works in storing information and the relationship with false beliefs.		
I have gotten a deeper understanding of how science works.		

 ## Value Cultivation

Read the text in Chinese and answer the questions.

陶友华又在"发呆"了。坐在电脑前，抱着胳膊，望着前方，甚至没注意到有人走近。

中国科学院长春应用化学研究所的同事都知道，陶友华一"发呆"，就是在构思新的前瞻领域的研究方向了。

要做就做有挑战性的课题，要做就做国家有需求的前瞻领域的课题。

这是陶友华一直坚持的信念。求学时是这样，2013年拒绝国外研究机构的邀请，义无反顾回到长春应化所后依然如此。

当前，国内外制造宇航服、医疗器械的高端高分子材料，都是以石化资源为原料，通过金属催化聚合的方法获得，但石化资源不可再生。以可再生资源为原料生产的氨基酸单体，经催化聚合后，可制备高端高分子材料，难点在于找不到合适的催化剂。

基于研究积累和国情省情，刚回国的陶友华将研究方向瞄准了这一世界性难题，提出发展弱键催化的氨基酸高分子合成的新策略，以更高效的方式实现从可再生资源到高端高分子材料的转化。

聚合釜不停歇运转，催化剂换了又换，氨基酸单体被催化了千万次，但实验一直停滞不前。

"陶老师，我想换个方向……"面对极高的难度，短期内又无产出的希望，团队曾有成员想放弃。

"搞科学哪那么容易，遇到困难是常事，咬牙坚持想办法解决它就好了。"陶友华召集大伙儿一起查文献、讨论解决思路。

2020年夏天，受团队成员一句"催化剂用硒修饰后，应该能够提高溶解性"的启发，陶友华再次调整催化剂……

两周后的一个晚上，实验室传来欢呼声："我们成功了！"

Extensive Reading 3

1. What do you learn from this story?

2. Which of the following quotes share the message of the story above? Choose all that apply. _____

   A. Science is nothing but perception. —Plato

   B. Men love to wonder, and that is the seed of science. —Ralph Waldo Emerson

   C. Science is organized knowledge. Wisdom is organized life. —Immanuel Kant

   D. The saddest aspect of life right now is that science gathers knowledge faster than society gathers wisdom. —Isaac Asimov

   E. 加快实现高水平科技自立自强，是推动高质量发展的必由之路。在激烈的国际竞争中，我们要开辟发展新领域新赛道、塑造发展新动能新优势，从根本上说，还是要依靠科技创新。我们能不能如期全面建成社会主义现代化强国，关键看科技自立自强。——2023年3月5日，习近平在参加十四届全国人大一次会议江苏代表团审议时的讲话

   F. 科学是老老实实的学问，不可能靠运气来创造发明，对一个问题的本质不了解，就是碰上机会也是枉然。入宝山而空手回，原因在此。——华罗庚

   G. 一个真正的科学家是忠于科学、热爱科学的。他热心科学，不是为名为利，而是求知，爱真理，为国家作贡献，为人民谋福利。——贝时璋

📖 Further Reading

1. *Thinking, Fast and Slow* by Daniel Kahneman
2. "Groundless Beliefs" by Alfred Ernest Mander
3. *A Discourse on the Method of Correctly Conducting One's Reason and Seeking Truth in the Sciences* by René Descartes (Oxford University Press)

Unit 5
Key Elements of Arguments: Definition

Extensive Reading 3

Mastering Critical Reading

A meaningful argument must begin with an agreement from all parties on what they are arguing about, so defining the key words before reasoning is essential. This is especially true when there are no unanimously accepted definitions, or the dispute stems from the understanding of these words.

Ambiguity or dispute about the understanding of some words arises easily from many factors, like polysemy, certain syntactic structures, and different interpretations of the context, and thus, readers run the risk of misunderstanding if writers fail to dispel the ambiguity or clarify the precise meaning of these words. Therefore, when writers assume that readers will be unfamiliar with these words, or some words are given new meanings in the current discussion, it is necessary to explain their intended meaning before reasoning.

To ensure an agreement on the nature and the basics of the argument, writers often take various approaches to clarify or highlight the meaning of vague or ambiguous terms or central concepts. The following list, which is by no means exhaustive, introduces some frequently read types of definitions.

■ **Definition from Dictionary**

Taking a definition from an authoritative dictionary is the simplest and most direct way to define a term since dictionaries are the best-accepted source of definitions. In many cases, the dictionary definition itself completely clarifies the meaning of a key word; however, in other cases, the dictionary definition alone, though authoritative, is not sufficient.

> **?** Do you often encounter dictionary definitions in your reading? When do you think it's necessary to give them? What are the possible limitations of definitions from the dictionary?

A dictionary definition often describes *the look or function or nature of the referent*. Sometimes, it also gives *a list of synonyms* or an explanation using equally obscure words, both of which cannot guarantee a full understanding for readers. Accordingly, a definition from a dictionary often appears together with some other types of explanation.

■ **Definition by Example**

Giving examples to illustrate terms can help readers get a more vivid understanding of the concepts in discussion, especially when those examples are familiar to readers. Examples may be factual, coming from real life, and hypothetical, designed for certain contexts. When the explanation in a dictionary or another source seems too broad or abstract, providing examples can be a good supplement to refine it, and thus make the definition, even the claim concerned, better understood and accepted.

However, defining by giving examples can be problematic sometimes. In some cases, examples may not always be at hand, especially for abstract terms. In other cases, it will be difficult to extract the commonplace from the many examples provided. Most of the time, the examples given may bear richer meanings or features than the term defined, so an example can make it difficult for readers to pin down the exact meaning of the term. All these risks determine that definition by example will be a good supplement to further elaborate a term, but it seldom goes alone.

> As is stated above, examples may be illustrative and lively, but they certainly have their own drawbacks. As a reader, what do you do when you have difficulty extracting the definition from the examples?
> As a writer, how would you choose examples to define a term?

■ Definition by Comparison and Contrast

It is often the case that a word goes hand in hand with another; the appearance of one inevitably reminds people of the other. More often than not, their meanings share much in common, though they have their own focus. In such cases, it is necessary to compare and/or contrast the term with other words of similar meanings in order to specify the subtle but important differences so that the readers understand precisely what the writer wants a given word to mean. For example, what is the difference between "knowledge" and "wisdom"?

> How will you define "comparison" or "contrast"? Will you compare these two terms to define them? How can we compare these two terms? How can we contrast them?

■ Definition by Word Origin

The word's original meaning may be helpful in understanding its current meaning or supporting the claim. Many English words come from other languages or have undergone much change in meaning over time. Tracing them back to their origin and combing through their semantic development help in justifying or supporting the writer's point. For example, that may hint at an argument for the positive understanding of "discrimination". However, again, the word's origin—called its *etymology*—by itself is by no means sufficient support or clarification of meaning.

> What are the historical semantic changes of the word "discrimination"? How can such changes possibly support a positive understanding of this word?

■ Definition by Stipulation

When there is no set definition for a term or the existing definition cannot satisfy the purpose of an argument, writers often provide a definition of their own, called a "stipulative definition", especially for

Extensive Reading 3

terms relating to values and abstract qualities. Although a stipulative definition may not focus on the standard usage of the term, it can clarify and fix the meaning of the term to that intended by the writer, thus ensuring an appropriate understanding of it and setting the basis for the discussion. However, the stipulated definition should be reasonable and clear to render it acceptable to readers.

> **?** Stipulative definitions are those designed by writers themselves, but they should be reasonable and clear. What do you think of the following definition of "netizen"? Is it acceptable? Why or why not?
> *By netizen, I mean anyone who has possible access to the Internet.*
> When do you think it is appropriate to give a stipulative definition?

■ **Many Other Ways**

This list of approaches to defining terms is neither exhaustive nor exclusive, so we may often encounter other means, or find various types together in a single text. For example, besides coming from the dictionary, a definition may also be taken from other authoritative sources. Other than providing the look, function, or nature of the referent, the definition may also describe typical features of the term defined. The writer can even design some analogies or metaphors to help explain the term.

❖ **Two Purposes of Defining**

Defining terms serves two purposes. Usually, specifying the definition of key terms is done to ensure an agreement on the understanding of them so as to provide a basis for further reasoning. However, sometimes, clarifying the meaning or understanding of a term or some terms can be the sole purpose of an argument.

💡 Enhancing Your Critical Reading (4)

In which ways are the words "infodemic" (in Text A, Unit 1) and "metaliteracy" (in Text B, Unit 1) defined?	
infodemic	
metaliteracy	

Unit 5 Key Elements of Arguments: Definition

Text A Crossing the Aegean Is "Traumatic". Your Bad Hair Day Isn't

Preparatory Work

Life certainly has its ups and downs for everyone. Sometimes those "downs" may seem so big and overwhelming that we think we can never make it through. But later, when we look back, sometimes those "downs" may seem trivial. Of course, some of them still hurt so much at the time that any recollection of them is painful. Do you have any "downs" that seemed too overwhelming at that time but seem trivial now? How did you come out of them? Would you share your experience? Maybe you can help others who are now suffering from such "downs".

My hard experience	The way I beat it

Reading the Text

> The word "trauma" has witnessed its increasing popularity nowadays. It seems that people are suffering more and more, and are more easily hurt than ever before. Is that so? How does Professor Haslam view this expansion of concept?

Crossing the Aegean Is "Traumatic". Your Bad Hair Day Isn't

Nicholas Haslam[1]

1 These days, "trauma" seems epidemic.

2 A group of Columbia Law School students felt the "traumatic effects" of the Michael Brown grand jury decision[2] so keenly, they argued, that they needed their finals postponed. A handful of Emory University students were "traumatized" by finding "Trump 2016" chalked on campus sidewalks. A young professor

chronicled his traumatizing graduate training, which included discrimination and job anxiety. And in an interview, a "trauma-sensitive yoga" instructor talked through her "hair trauma": "I grew up with really curly, frizzy hair in Miami, Florida. When you're 13, a bad hair day is overwhelming," she said. "Even though I would never compare that to someone who was abused, it's an experience that shaped my identity and, at the time, was intolerable."

3   These aren't isolated incidents. Trauma is being used to describe an increasingly wide array of events. By today's standards, it can be caused by a microaggression, reading something offensive without a trigger warning or even watching upsetting news unfold on television. As one blogger wrote, "Trauma now seems to be pretty much anything that bothers anyone, in any way, ever."

4   This is not a mere terminological fad. It reflects a steady expansion of the word's meaning by psychiatrists and the culture at large. And its promiscuous use has worrying implications. When we describe misfortune, sadness or even pain as trauma, we redefine our experience. Using the word "trauma" turns every event into a catastrophe, leaving us helpless, broken and unable to move on.

5   Like democracy, alarm clocks and the Olympics, we owe "trauma" to the ancient Greeks. For them, trauma was a severe physical injury; the word shares its linguistic root with terms for breaking apart and bruising. Of course, doctors still use "trauma" to describe physical harm. But more and more, we understand the term in a second way—as an emotional injury rather than a physical wound.

6   This shift started in the late 19th century, when neurologists such as Jean-Martin Charcot[3] and Sigmund Freud[4] posited that some neuroses were caused by deeply distressing experiences. The idea was revolutionary—a dawning recognition that shattered minds could be explained psychologically as well as biologically.

7   Ideas about psychological trauma continued to take shape in the 20th century, but the physical sense still dominated. In 1952, the first edition of *The Diagnostic and Statistical Manual of Mental Disorders*, which catalogues psychological illnesses, mentioned the term only in relation to brain injuries caused by force or electric shock.

8   By 1980, that had changed. The DSM's third edition recognized post-traumatic stress disorder for the first time, though the definition of a "traumatic event" was relatively focused—it had to be "outside the range of usual human experience" and severe enough to "evoke significant symptoms of distress in almost everyone". The DSM-III's authors argued that common experiences such as chronic illness,

Refugees crossing the Aegean to the island of Lesbos, seeking a new life.

marital conflict and bereavement did not meet the definition.

9   Later editions of psychiatry's "bible"—really more like a field guide to the species of human misery—loosened the definition further, expanding it to incorporate indirect experiences such as violent assaults of family members and friends, along with "developmentally inappropriate sexual experiences" and occasions when people witness serious injury or death. One study found that 19 events qualified as traumatic in the DSM-IV; just 14 would have qualified in the revised edition of the DSM-III.

10   This broadening of the definition was justified in part by the finding that people who were indirectly exposed to stressful events could develop PTSD symptoms. Even so, researchers became concerned that elastic concepts of trauma "risk trivializing the suffering of those exposed to catastrophic life events". As psychologist Stephen Joseph explained in a 2011 interview, "The DSM over-medicalizes human experience. Things which are relatively common, relatively normal, are turned into psychiatric disorders."

11   An Army National Guard medic argued in *Scientific American* that "clinicians aren't separating the few who really have PTSD from those who are experiencing things like depression or anxiety or social and reintegration problems, or who are just taking some time getting over it". This, he worried, would lead to people being "pulled into a treatment and disability regime that will mire them in a self-fulfilling vision of a brain rewired, a psyche permanently haunted".

12   That hasn't stopped definition expansion. The federal Substance Abuse and Mental Health Services Administration, for example, now says trauma can involve ongoing circumstances rather than a distinct event—no serious threat to life or limb necessary. Trauma, by the agency's definition, doesn't even have to be outside normal experience. No wonder clinicians increasingly identify such common experiences as uncomplicated childbirth, marital infidelity, wisdom-tooth extraction and hearing offensive jokes as possible causes of PTSD.

13   This thinking has seeped into our culture as well. The word "trauma" itself has exploded in popularity in recent decades. A search of the 500 billion words that make up the Google Books database reveals that "trauma" appeared at four times the rate in 2005 as in 1965. According to Google Trends, interest in the word has grown by a third in the past five years.

14   How to explain this change? For one thing, the broadening of "trauma" coincides with other psychological shifts, such as a sense that our life outcomes are out of our control. According to one study, young people increasingly believe that their destinies are determined by luck, fate or powerful people besides themselves. People who hold these beliefs are more likely to feel helpless and unable to manage stress. Trauma is a way to explain life's problems as someone else's fault.

15   A second explanation can be found in my work on "concept creep". In recent decades, several psychological concepts have undergone semantic inflation. The definitions of abuse, addiction, bullying,

mental disorder and prejudice have all expanded to include a broad range of phenomena. This reflects a growing sensitivity to harm in Western societies. By broadening the reach of these concepts—recognizing emotional manipulation as abuse, the spreading of rumors as bullying and increasingly mild conditions as psychiatric problems—we identify more people as victims of harm. We express a well-intentioned unwillingness to accept things that were previously tolerated, but we also risk over-sensitivity: defining relatively innocuous phenomena as serious problems that require outside intervention. The expansion of the concept of trauma runs the same risk.

16   All of this is problematic. The way we interpret an experience affects how we respond to it. Interpreting adversity as trauma makes it seem calamitous and likely to have lasting effects. When an affliction is seen as traumatic, it becomes something overwhelming—something that breaks us, that is likely to produce post-traumatic symptoms and that requires professional intervention. Research shows that people who tend to interpret negative events as catastrophic and long-lasting are more susceptible to post-traumatic reactions. Perceiving challenging life experiences as traumas may therefore increase our vulnerability to them.

17   Our choice of language matters. A famous study by cognitive psychologist Elizabeth Loftus illustrates why. Loftus showed people films of traffic accidents and asked them to judge the speed of the cars involved, using subtly varying instructions. Different study participants were asked how fast the cars were going when they "smashed" "collided" "bumped" "hit" or "contacted" each other. Despite watching the very same collisions, people judged the cars to be traveling 28 percent faster when they were described as "smashing" rather than "contacting".

18   To define all adversities as traumas is akin to seeing all collisions as smashes. People collide with misfortune all the time: Sometimes it smashes them, but often they merely make contact.

19   Another fine invention of the ancient Greeks was stoicism. Contrary to popular opinion, the stoics did not think we should simply endure or brush off adversity. Rather, they believed that we should confront suffering with composure and rational judgment. We should all cultivate stoic wisdom to judge the difference between traumas that can break us apart and normal adversities that we can overcome.

(Source: *The Washington Post,* August 14, 2016.)

Notes

1. **Nick Haslam** is a professor of psychology at the University of Melbourne. His research interests are in personality, social and clinical psychology, and he has published 11 books and about 300 articles or book chapters in these and related areas.
2. A **grand jury** decided not to indict Darren Wilson in Ferguson, Missouri, United States, for any crimes related to the death of **Michael Brown** in August 2014. Wilson, a white police officer, shot and killed Brown, an unarmed black teenager, in an August 9 incident, which has stoked anger and debate in

Ferguson and beyond.

3. **Jean-Martin Charcot** (1825—1893) was a French neurologist and professor of anatomical pathology. He is regarded as a founder of modern neurology, the father of French neurology, and one of the world's pioneers of neurology.

4. **Sigmund Freud** (1856—1939) was an Austrian neurologist, medical doctor, psychologist, and influential thinker of the early twentieth century. He was best known for developing the theories and techniques of psychoanalysis.

 Remembering and Understanding

Activity 1 Trace the Change of Meaning

In the article, the author traces the expansion of the meaning of the word "trauma". What are the meanings of this word? Find some examples for each definition from the text. You can also provide some examples by yourself according to the definitions.

Time of origin:
Original meaning:
Possible examples:

⬇

Time for beginning of the change:
Trigger for the change:
Significance of the shift:
Possible examples:

⬇

First edition of DSM in 1952
Scope of meaning:
Possible examples:

⬇

Extensive Reading 3

(continued)

DSM-III by 1980
Scope of meaning:
Possible examples:

⬇

DSM-IV
Scope of meaning:
Possible examples:

⬇

Substance abuse and mental health services administration
Scope of meaning:
Possible examples:

Activity 2 Answer the Following Questions

Besides listing the changing meanings of the word, this text covers more on this issue. Answer the following questions based on the information provided in the text.

1. How widely is the word "trauma" used now?

   _____
   _____

2. What are the reasons for this semantic broadening?

   _____
   _____

3. How problematic is this expansion?

   _____
   _____

4. How can this problem be solved?

   _____
   _____

Unit 5 Key Elements of Arguments: Definition

 Reasoning and Analyzing

Answer the following questions.

1. What does the author mean by the title?

2. What is the claim, or thesis, of this article?

3. What is "concept creep", according to the text? What is the effect of the author's mentioning his work on "concept creep" here?

4. What kind of people are more likely to get hurt by the increasingly broad scope of "traumatic" experience?

5. Why does the author trace back so far into ancient Greece for the original meaning of this word?

6. Why does the author base his argument about word definition mainly on *The Diagnostic and Statistical Manual of Mental Disorders*, instead of a dictionary?

7. In the text, the author proposes some ways to solve this problem. What does the author think of the solutions?

8. Which techniques for defining does the author take in this article? How effective are they?

Extensive Reading 3

 Reflecting and Creating

Topics for discussion and writing.

1. As the world develops and our knowledge of the world expands, man's experience naturally becomes broader and more diverse. In such a context, do you think it is acceptable for words to expand in meaning? What may be the merits and demerits of meaning expansion of words?

2. Do you think the name of something or the definition of a term can really affect how we see it or how we respond to it? If yes, can you give some examples to illustrate the power of language? If no, what may affect us?

3. Societies are now developing at a faster and faster pace, and people are facing more and more challenges and pressures. In this modern life, how can people tackle pressures and unpleasant experiences to keep themselves from getting hurt by them?

Text B   Knowledge and Wisdom (Excerpt)

 Preparatory Work

Do you still remember Socrates's definition of "wisdom" (in Text A, Unit 3)? Do you think you are a wise person in Socrates's sense?

According to you, what kind of people can be called "knowledgeable", "intelligent", and "wise"? Are you a knowledgeable person? An intelligent person? A wise person? Give some examples of a knowledgeable person, an intelligent person, and a wise person. What kind of person do you want to be?

My definition of ...	Examples of ...
knowledgeable person	
intelligent person	
wise person	

112

Unit 5 Key Elements of Arguments: Definition

Reading the Text

> According to Socrates, the only true wisdom is in knowing you know nothing. Would Bertrand Russell share this understanding of wisdom? What's the relation between knowledge and wisdom?

Knowledge and Wisdom (Excerpt)

Bertrand Russell[1]

1   Most people would agree that, although our age far surpasses all previous ages in knowledge, there has been no correlative increase in wisdom. But agreement ceases as soon as we attempt to define "wisdom" and consider means of promoting it. I want to ask first what wisdom is, and then what can be done to teach it.

Source: news.sohu.com/a/505169007_250147

2   There are, I think, several factors that contribute to wisdom. Of these I should put first a sense of proportion: the capacity to take account of all the important factors in a problem and to attach to each its due weight. This has become more difficult than it used to be owing to the extent and complexity of the specialized knowledge required of various kinds of technicians. Suppose, for example, that you are engaged in research in scientific medicine. The work is difficult and is likely to absorb the whole of your intellectual energy. You have not time to consider the effect which your discoveries or inventions may have outside the field of medicine. You succeed (let us say), as modern medicine has succeeded, in enormously lowering the infant death-rate, not only in Europe and America, but also in Asia and Africa. This has the entirely unintended result of making the food supply inadequate and lowering the standard of life in the most populous parts of the world. To take an even more spectacular example, which is in everybody's mind at the present time: You study the composition of the atom from a disinterested desire for knowledge, and incidentally place in the hands of powerful lunatics the means of destroying the human race. In such ways the pursuit of knowledge may become harmful unless it is combined with wisdom; and wisdom in the sense of

comprehensive vision is not necessarily present in specialists in the pursuit of knowledge.

3   Comprehensiveness alone, however, is not enough to constitute wisdom. There must be, also, a certain awareness of the ends of human life. This may be illustrated by the study of history. Many eminent historians have done more harm than good because they viewed facts through the distorting medium of their own passions. Hegel[2] had a philosophy of history which did not suffer from any lack of comprehensiveness, since it started from the earliest times and continued into an indefinite future. But the chief lesson of history which he sought to inculcate was that from the year 400AD down to his own time Germany had been the most important nation and the standard-bearer of progress in the world. Perhaps one could stretch the comprehensiveness that constitutes wisdom to include not only intellect but also feeling. It is by no means uncommon to find men whose knowledge is wide but whose feelings are narrow. Such men lack what I call wisdom.

4   It is not only in public ways, but in private life equally, that wisdom is needed. It is needed in the choice of ends to be pursued and in emancipation from personal prejudice. Even an end which it would be noble to pursue if it were attainable may be pursued unwisely if it is inherently impossible of achievement. Many men in past ages devoted their lives to a search for the philosopher's stone and the elixir of life. No doubt, if they could have found them, they would have conferred great benefits upon mankind, but as it was their lives were wasted. To descend to less heroic matters, consider the case of two men, Mr A and Mr B, who hate each other and, through mutual hatred, bring each other to destruction. Suppose you go to Mr A and say, "Why do you hate Mr B?" He will no doubt give you an appalling list of Mr B's vices, partly true, partly false. And now suppose you go to Mr B. He will give you an exactly similar list of Mr A's vices with an equal admixture of truth and falsehood. Suppose you now come back to Mr A and say, 'You will be surprised to learn that Mr B says the same things about you as you say about him', and you go to Mr B and make a similar speech. The first effect, no doubt, will be to increase their mutual hatred, since each will be so horrified by the other's injustice. But perhaps, if you have sufficient patience and sufficient persuasiveness, you may succeed in convincing each that the other has only the normal share of human wickedness, and that their enmity is harmful to both. If you can do this, you will have instilled some fragment of wisdom.

5   I think the essence of wisdom is emancipation, as far as possible, from the tyranny of the here and now. We cannot help the egoism of our senses. Sight and sound and touch are bound up with our own bodies and cannot be impersonal. Our emotions start similarly from ourselves. An infant feels hunger or discomfort, and is unaffected except by his own physical condition. Gradually with the years, his horizon widens, and, in proportion as his thoughts and feelings become less personal and less concerned with his own physical states, he achieves growing wisdom. This is of course a matter of degree. No one can view the world with complete impartiality; and if anyone could, he would hardly be able to remain alive. But it is possible to make a

continual approach towards impartiality, on the one hand, by knowing things somewhat remote in time or space, and on the other hand, by giving to such things their due weight in our feelings. It is this approach towards impartiality that constitutes growth in wisdom.

(Source: "Knowledge and Wisdom" in *Portraits from Memory and Other Essays*, 2021.)

Notes

1. **Bertrand Arthur William Russell** (1872—1970) was a British philosopher, logician, mathematician, writer, historian, social critic, political activist, and Nobel laureate. He is best known for his work in mathematical logic and analytic philosophy. In 1950, Russell was awarded the Nobel Prize in Literature "in recognition of his varied and significant writings in which he champions humanitarian ideals and freedom of thought".
2. **Georg Wilhelm Friedrich Hegel** (1770—1831) was a German philosopher of the late Enlightenment, the main representative of nineteenth-century German Idealism, and one of the major thinkers in the history of Western philosophy.

Remembering and Understanding

Activity 1 Answer the Following Questions

1. What would most people agree about and disagree about regarding knowledge and wisdom, according to the text?
   _____
   _____

2. What do the examples of study in scientific medicine and composition of the atom in Para. 2 illustrate?
   _____
   _____

3. What does the author think of Hegel? Why does he refer to Hegel here?
   _____
   _____

4. Why is wisdom also needed in private life?
   _____
   _____

5. At the end of Para. 4, the author concludes that "If you can do this, you will have instilled some fragment of wisdom". What does "this" refer to? By doing so, whose wisdom will grow?

Extensive Reading 3

6. What is "the egoism of our senses" in Para. 5? Why can't we "help the egoism of our senses"?

7. What does the author think of impartiality? How can we acquire it?

Activity 2 What Is Wisdom?

In the text, the author elaborates on several factors that contribute to wisdom. What are those factors?

Summarize a concise definition of "wisdom" based on the factors proposed by the author.

📝 Reasoning and Analyzing

Answer the following questions.

1. Why has acquiring a sense of proportion become more difficult than it used to be (Para. 2)? How does the author support or explain this point?

Unit 5 Key Elements of Arguments: Definition

2. The first factor the author puts forward is a sense of proportion. What is its relation with comprehensiveness?
   _____
   _____

3. What does the author mean by "the ends of human life" in Para. 3? How is "a certain awareness of the ends of human life" related to "feeling"?
   _____
   _____

4. What does the author think of the search for the philosopher's stone and the elixir of life? Why? How does this example contribute to the author's point in this paragraph?
   _____
   _____

5. Why is emancipation from the tyranny of the here and now the essence of wisdom?
   _____
   _____

6. Immediately after this excerpt, the author raises the question, "Can wisdom in this sense be taught?" What do you think the author's answer to this question would be? What clue can you find in this excerpt?
   _____
   _____

7. Which ways does the author employ to explain the meaning of wisdom in this article? How effective are they?
   _____
   _____

Reflecting and Creating

Topics for discussion and writing.

1. The article is entitled "Knowledge and Wisdom". If you were to write an article with this title, what content would you include? How would you develop your ideas? What do you think of your arrangement of the article as compared with this one?

2. As the author said, "The pursuit of knowledge may become harmful unless it is combined with wisdom" (Para. 2). Do you think wisdom alone can prevent or keep the pursuit of knowledge from becoming harmful? If yes, how can wisdom achieve that? If no, what other efforts are needed to prevent or solve this problem?

Extensive Reading 3

3. At the beginning of his essay, the author introduced that he would discuss, besides "what wisdom is", also "what can be done to teach it". What do you predict his measures would be in teaching wisdom? How do you think college education can contribute to the cultivation of wisdom? How can other stages of education contribute to that?

Summary

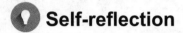

Self-reflection

Fill out the checklist.

Area	Yes / No?	Notes / Comment
I know the merits and demerits of the dictionary definition, and how to use it.		
I know the merits and demerits of definition by example, and how to use it.		
I know the merits and demerits of definition by comparison and contrast, and how to use it.		
I know the merits and demerits of definition by word origin, and how to use it.		
I know the merits and demerits of definition by stipulation, and how to use it.		
I have gotten a deeper understanding of the meaning of "trauma" and the significance of the word's meaning.		
I now know more about the features of wisdom and its importance.		

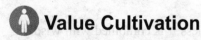

Activity 1 Quotes Exploration

Match the quotes with the people who said them, listed below. Please note that there are two extra options you do not need to use.

1. The whole problem with the world is that fools and fanatics are always so certain of themselves, and wiser people so full of doubts.
2. Beware of false knowledge; it is more dangerous than ignorance.
3. Life is far too important a thing ever to talk seriously about.
4. Give me a lever long enough and a fulcrum on which to place it, and I shall move the world.
5. All our knowledge begins with the senses, proceeds then to the understanding, and ends with reason. There is nothing higher than reason.

A. Ernest Hemingway   B. Archimedes   C. Oscar Wilde   D. George Bernard Shaw
E. Bertrand Russell   F. Isaac Newton   G. Immanuel Kant

Activity 2 Translation of Epigrams

The following are the English translation of two Chinese epigrams. Try to make out the original Chinese version of each epigram. What message does each piece carry?

1. Nature's ways are constant. They did not exist because Yao was on the throne or disappear because Jie was the ruler. —*Xunzi*

Chinese version: _____

The message: _____

2. What is known without thinking is the innate knowledge of goodness. —*Mencius*

Chinese version: _____

The message: _____

 # Further Reading

1. "The Creeping Concept of Trauma" by Nick Haslam & Melanie J. McGrath
2. *The Conquest of Happiness* by Bertrand Russell
3. "Of Adversity" by Francis Bacon

Unit 6
Key Elements of Arguments: Claim

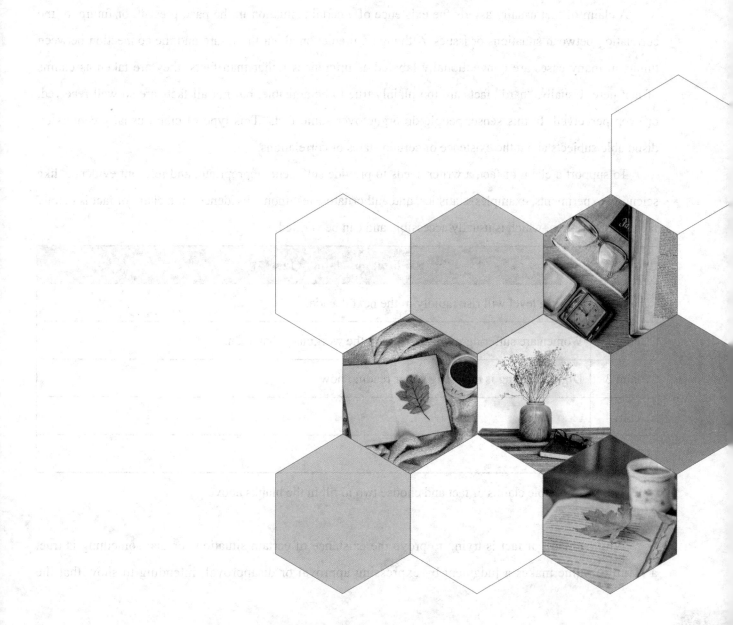

Extensive Reading 3

Mastering Critical Reading

The claim, a central element of any argument, is what the argument asserts or attempts to prove. It answers the question, "What is your point?" In argumentative writing, the claim is the writer's main idea or thesis. It can be presented directly at the beginning of the writing (typically preferable) or the end, but implied claims are not rare. The content of claims may vary greatly among writings, and the classification also varies very much due to different criteria and perspectives. In our discussion, we consider claims falling broadly into three categories: claims of fact, of value, and of policy.

■ **Claim of Fact**

A claim of fact usually asserts the existence of a certain situation in the past, present, or future, or the correlation between situations or issues. Although a prediction about the future and the connection between things in many cases are conventionally labeled as inferences rather than facts, they are taken as claims of fact here. Usually, "hard" facts are too plainly true to be arguable, but not all facts are so well received, or even perceived. In this sense, people do argue over some facts. This type of claim usually centers on disputable subjects about the existence of certain states or correlations.

To support a claim of fact, a writer needs to provide sufficient, appropriate, and relevant evidence, like scientific experiments, examples, statistics, and authoritative testimony. Evidence for a claim of fact is mainly factual information, which is usually accessible and can be verified.

Examples of claim of fact	
Claim 1	The sea level will rise rapidly in the next decade.
Claim 2	Women are suffering more pressure in the workplace than men.
Claim 3	Digital reading is replacing paper reading now.
Claim 4	
Claim 5	

Think of possible claims of fact and choose two to fill in the blanks above.

■ **Claim of Value**

While a claim of fact is trying to prove the existence of certain situations or that something is true, a claim of value makes a judgment by expressing approval or disapproval, intending to show that the conditions or actions in discussion are right or wrong, good or bad, worthwhile or undesirable, etc. Value claims are more easily found in arguments about moral, ethical, and aesthetic judgments. However, some claims of value, those which are simply expressions of personal tastes, likes, dislikes, preferences, or prejudices, may not lead to meaningful arguments if they are not well-reasoned and supported.

A good argument of judgment calls for careful reasoning, appropriate evidence, and well-received assumptions to back it up. Claims of value are often built on other value statements. For example, the claim that abortion is wrong is mainly based on the value of equal right to life that should be granted to every person, including a fetus. So, for claims of value, critical readers, besides evaluating the reasoning and support of the argument, will also keep asking: What are the standards or criteria for making the judgment? What are the embedded values that this judgment is based on? Are they acceptable to me or general readers?

	Examples of claim of value
Claim 1	*Jane Eyre* is one of the best novels in English literature.
Claim 2	Keeping schools closed will do more harm than good.
Claim 3	Discussion-based classes are better than lecture-based ones.
Claim 4	
Claim 5	

Think of possible claims of value and choose two to fill in the blanks above.

■ **Claim of Policy**

A claim of policy proposes actions, measures, or changes to an existing policy or situation in order to solve problems. It often starts from a certain situation that the writer presents as problematic, and then advocates the adoption of policies or courses of action—what we, certain people, or the government ought or ought not to do, what should or should not happen—in order to best solve the problem.

It is natural and understandable, therefore, that when reading claims of policy, we may often encounter a mixture of claims, policies, and values, or even all three. To solve a problem, after all, a writer must first convince the audience that there **is** a problem. Especially in a long and complicated argument, a writer may start from a factual claim to show that a condition exists, and then prove that the present condition is undesirable. This process naturally leads to the policy and the attempt to persuade the audience that the solution proposed will best solve the problem.

Extensive Reading 3

Examples of claim of policy	
Claim 1	The United States should outlaw gun ownership right now.
Claim 2	Consumerism should be promoted to save the economy.
Claim 3	The time required for primary school should be shortened to five years.
Claim 4	
Claim 5	

Think of possible claims of policy and choose two to fill in the blanks above.

💡 Enhancing Your Critical Reading (5)

Identify texts that carry claims of fact, of value, and of policy, respectively, from all the texts you have read in this textbook up to this point. Give the titles in the following table. Can you always make a clear-cut division between them?

Claim of fact	
Claim of value	
Claim of policy	

Unit 6 Key Elements of Arguments: Claim

Text A Letter from Birmingham Jail (Excerpt)

Preparatory Work

Activity 1 Who Are They?

The following text is written by Martin Luther King Jr. Have you read his speech "I Have a Dream"? How much do you know about him and his contribution?

In the text, he refers to many other people, like Jesus, Martin Luther, John Bunyan, and Thomas Jefferson. How much do you know about them? Collect information about people in the following table and give a brief introduction to each.

In the text, the following people are all regarded as "extremists" in certain sense. In which sense do you think they are possibly regarded as "extremists"?

People	Brief introduction	The way they are regarded as "extremists"
Martin Luther King Jr.		
Jesus		
Amos		
Paul the Apostle		
Martin Luther		
John Bunyan		
Abraham Lincoln		
Thomas Jefferson		

Extensive Reading 3

Activity 2 What Would You Call Them?

Text A is about black people's struggle for their civil rights in the United States. What would you call the black people now? The author of this article used the word "Negro". Would you use the term now? How does language matter in this case?

What words would you use?	
Has there been any change in the meaning of "Negro"?	
How does language matter here?	

Reading the Text

> Responding to an open letter denouncing him and his demonstrations by eight clergymen, Martin Luther King Jr. wrote a letter in reply from Birmingham jail where he was imprisoned. In this excerpt from the letter, King expressed his strong disappointment toward the white moderate, but did he stop at expressing emotions?

Letter from Birmingham Jail (Excerpt)

Martin Luther King Jr.[1]

Martin Luther King Jr. Photo: Politified

source: www.woodlandsjournal.com/2017/01/16/10-interesting-facts-about-dr-martin-luther-king-jr/

Unit 6　Key Elements of Arguments: Claim

¹　...I must confess that over the past few years I have been gravely disappointed with the white moderate. I have almost reached the regrettable conclusion that the Negro's great stumbling block in his stride toward freedom is not the White Citizen's Counciler or the Ku Klux Klanner, but the white moderate, who is more devoted to "order" than to justice; who prefers a negative peace which is the absence of tension to a positive peace which is the presence of justice; who constantly says: "I agree with you in the goal you seek, but I cannot agree with your methods of direct action"; who paternalistically believes he can set the timetable for another man's freedom; who lives by a mythical concept of time and who constantly advises the Negro to wait for a "more convenient season". Shallow understanding from people of good will is more frustrating than absolute misunderstanding from people of ill will. Lukewarm acceptance is much more bewildering than outright rejection.

²　I had hoped that the white moderate would understand that law and order exist for the purpose of establishing justice and that when they fail in this purpose they become the dangerously structured dams that block the flow of social progress. I had hoped that the white moderate would understand that the present tension in the South is a necessary phase of the transition from an obnoxious negative peace, in which the Negro passively accepted his unjust plight, to a substantive and positive peace, in which all men will respect the dignity and worth of human personality. Actually, we who engage in nonviolent direct action are not the creators of tension. We merely bring to the surface the hidden tension that is already alive. We bring it out in the open, where it can be seen and dealt with. Like a boil that can never be cured so long as it is covered up but must be opened with all its ugliness to the natural medicines of air and light, injustice must be exposed, with all the tension its exposure creates, to the light of human conscience and the air of national opinion before it can be cured.

³　In your statement you assert that our actions, even though peaceful, must be condemned because they precipitate violence. But is this a logical assertion? Isn't this like condemning a robbed man because his possession of money precipitated the evil act of robbery? Isn't this like condemning Socrates because his unswerving commitment to truth and his philosophical inquiries precipitated the act by the misguided populace in which they made him drink hemlock? Isn't this like condemning Jesus because his unique God-consciousness and never-ceasing devotion to God's will precipitated the evil act of crucifixion? We must come to see that, as the federal courts have consistently affirmed, it is wrong to urge an individual to cease his efforts to gain his basic constitutional rights because the quest may precipitate violence. Society must protect the robbed and punish the robber.

⁴　I had also hoped that the white moderate would reject the myth concerning time in relation to the struggle for freedom. I have just received a letter from a white brother in Texas. He writes: "All Christians know that the colored people will receive equal rights eventually, but it is possible that you are in too great a

religious hurry. It has taken Christianity almost two thousand years to accomplish what it has. The teachings of Christ take time to come to earth." Such an attitude stems from a tragic misconception of time, from the strangely rational notion that there is something in the very flow of time that will inevitably cure all ills. Actually, time itself is neutral; it can be used either destructively or constructively. More and more I feel that the people of ill will have used time much more effectively than have the people of good will. We will have to repent in this generation not merely for the hateful words and actions of the bad people but for the appalling silence of the good people. Human progress never rolls in on wheels of inevitability; it comes through the tireless efforts of men willing to be co-workers with God, and without this hard work, time itself becomes an ally of the forces of social stagnation. We must use time creatively, in the knowledge that the time is always ripe to do right. Now is the time to make real the promise of democracy and transform our pending national elegy into a creative psalm of brotherhood. Now is the time to lift our national policy from the quicksand of racial injustice to the solid rock of human dignity.

5   You speak of our activity in Birmingham as extreme. At first I was rather disappointed that fellow clergymen would see my nonviolent efforts as those of an extremist. I began thinking about the fact that I stand in the middle of two opposing forces in the Negro community. One is a force of complacency, made up in part of Negroes who, as a result of long years of oppression, are so drained of self-respect and a sense of "somebodiness" that they have adjusted to segregation; and in part of a few middle class Negroes who, because of a degree of academic and economic security and because in some ways they profit by segregation, have become insensitive to the problems of the masses. The other force is one of bitterness and hatred, and it comes perilously close to advocating violence. It is expressed in the various black nationalist groups that are springing up across the nation, the largest and best-known being Elijah Muhammad's[2] Muslim movement. Nourished by the Negro's frustration over the continued existence of racial discrimination, this movement is made up of people who have lost faith in America, who have absolutely repudiated Christianity, and who have concluded that the white man is an incorrigible "devil".

6   I have tried to stand between these two forces, saying that we need emulate neither the "do-nothingism" of the complacent nor the hatred and despair of the black nationalist. For there is the more excellent way of love and nonviolent protest. I am grateful to God that, through the influence of the Negro church, the way of nonviolence became an integral part of our struggle.

7   If this philosophy had not emerged, by now many streets of the South would, I am convinced, be flowing with blood. And I am further convinced that if our white brothers dismiss as "rabble-rousers" and "outside agitators" those of us who employ nonviolent direct action, and if they refuse to support our nonviolent efforts, millions of Negroes will, out of frustration and despair, seek solace and security in black-nationalist ideologies a development that would inevitably lead to a frightening racial nightmare.

8   Oppressed people cannot remain oppressed forever. The yearning for freedom eventually manifests itself, and that is what has happened to the American Negro. Something within has reminded him of his birthright of freedom, and something without has reminded him that it can be gained. Consciously or unconsciously, he has been caught up by the Zeitgeist, and with his black brothers of Africa and his brown and yellow brothers of Asia, South America and the Caribbean, the United States Negro is moving with a sense of great urgency toward the promised land of racial justice. If one recognizes this vital urge that has engulfed the Negro community, one should readily understand why public demonstrations are taking place. The Negro has many pent-up resentments and latent frustrations, and he must release them. So let him march; let him make prayer pilgrimages to the city hall; let him go on freedom rides—and try to understand why he must do so. If his repressed emotions are not released in nonviolent ways, they will seek expression through violence; this is not a threat but a fact of history. So I have not said to my people: "Get rid of your discontent." Rather, I have tried to say that this normal and healthy discontent can be channeled into the creative outlet of nonviolent direct action. And now this approach is being termed extremist.

Encyclopædia Britannica, https://www.britannica.com/summary/Martin-Luther-King-Jr-Timeline#/media/1/318311/250030

9   But though I was initially disappointed at being categorized as an extremist, as I continued to think about the matter I gradually gained a measure of satisfaction from the label. Was not Jesus an extremist for love: "Love your enemies, bless them that curse you, do good to them that hate you, and pray for them which despitefully use you, and persecute you." Was not Amos an extremist for justice: "Let justice roll down like waters and righteousness like an ever-flowing stream." Was not Paul an extremist for the Christian gospel: "I bear in my body the marks of the Lord Jesus." Was not Martin Luther an extremist: "Here I stand; I cannot do otherwise, so help me God." And John Bunyan: "I will stay in jail to the end of my days before I make a butchery of my conscience." And Abraham Lincoln: "This nation cannot survive half slave and half free." And Thomas Jefferson: "We hold these truths to be self-evident, that all men are created equal..."

So the question is not whether we will be extremists, but what kind of extremists we will be. Will we be extremists for hate or for love? Will we be extremists for the preservation of injustice or for the extension of justice? In that dramatic scene on Calvary's[3] hill three men were crucified. We must never forget that all three were crucified for the same crime—the crime of extremism. Two were extremists for immorality, and thus fell below their environment. The other, Jesus Christ, was an extremist for love, truth and goodness, and thereby rose above his environment. Perhaps the South, the nation and the world are in dire need of creative extremists.

10   I had hoped that the white moderate would see this need. Perhaps I was too optimistic; perhaps I expected too much. I suppose I should have realized that few members of the oppressor race can understand the deep groans and passionate yearnings of the oppressed race, and still fewer have the vision to see that injustice must be rooted out by strong, persistent and determined action. I am thankful, however, that some of our white brothers in the South have grasped the meaning of this social revolution and committed themselves to it. They are still too few in quantity, but they are big in quality. Some—such as Ralph McGill, Lillian Smith, Harry Golden, James McBride Dabbs, Ann Braden and Sarah Patton Boyle—have written about our struggle in eloquent and prophetic terms. Others have marched with us down nameless streets of the South. They have languished in filthy, roach-infested jails, suffering the abuse and brutality of policemen who view them as "dirty nigger lovers". Unlike so many of their moderate brothers and sisters, they have recognized the urgency of the moment and sensed the need for powerful "action" antidotes to combat the disease of segregation.

(Source: "Letter from Birmingham Jail" in *Why We Can't Wait*, 2010.)

Notes

1. **Martin Luther King Jr.** (1929—1968) was a social activist and Baptist minister who led the civil rights movement in the United States from the mid-1950s until his assassination in 1968. King was awarded the Nobel Peace Prize in 1964 and is commemorated by Martin Luther King Jr. Day, a US federal holiday on the third Monday in January, since 1986.
2. **Elijah Muhammad** (1897—1975), original name Elijah Poole, was a leader of the black separatist religious movement known as the Nation of Islam (sometimes called Black Muslims) in the United States from 1934 until his death in 1975.
3. **Calvary**, also known as Golgotha, is the name of a skull-shaped hill in ancient Jerusalem where Jesus was crucified.

Unit 6 Key Elements of Arguments: Claim

 Remembering and Understanding

Activity 1 Answer the Following Questions

1. How does the author feel about the white moderate? Why?

2. What does the author mean by "negative peace" and "positive peace"?

3. According to the author, what may be points of agreement and disagreement between the white moderate and King (and King's people)?

4. As is said at the end of Para. 1, "Shallow understanding from people of good will is more frustrating than absolute misunderstanding from people of ill will." Of these two types, what kind of people is the white moderate as distinguished here? What kind of people are the White Citizen's Counciler and the Ku Klux Klanner?

5. What does King think of tension? In which way is it like a boil?

6. Para. 3 ends with, "Society must protect the robbed and punish the robber." To whom do you think "the robbed" refers, and who is "the robber" referred to in King's context? In which way are they like their referents?

7. What is "the myth concerning time"(Para.4)? How can this myth be rejected?

8. Why was King disappointed at first when his efforts were regarded as those of an extremist? What was the situation like in "the Negro community" at that time? Why would some African Americans feel complacent?

131

Extensive Reading 3

9. What is "this philosophy" at the beginning of Para. 7? If it was not for "this philosophy," what would happen?

10. What does the mentioning of Zeitgeist in Para. 8 imply?

11. Why does the author say he was "too optimistic" in Para. 10?

12. Does the term *white moderate* include all white people?

Activity 2 Outline the Text

Write a structured outline of the text based on your understanding of this excerpt.

Reasoning and Analyzing

Answer the following questions.

1. As was introduced, this excerpt is taken from a letter in reply to the criticism leveled at King and his actions. What criticism can you identify from the excerpt?

Unit 6　Key Elements of Arguments: Claim

2. What is the logic behind the clergymen's condemnation of King's actions in Para. 3? What's the logic behind King's examples? Are they reasonable and acceptable?
   _____
   _____

3. What's wrong with the ideas in the letter in Para. 4? How does King respond to this letter? What do you think of those ideas?
   _____
   _____

4. What would be the definition of "extremist" as used by the white clergymen? What would be its definition as used by King? How does King clarify the meaning of this word in the text?
   _____
   _____

5. What rhetorical devices does the author use? What are the effects of using these rhetorical devices?
   _____
   _____

6. What strategies does the author apply to develop and support his major ideas in the text?
   _____
   _____

7. Who do you think is the intended audience of this writing?
   _____
   _____

8. What is the writing purpose of this letter according to this excerpt?
   _____
   _____

9. What kind of claim would you classify this text into? Is it a claim of fact, of value, or of policy? Why?
   _____
   _____

◀ Reflecting and Creating

Topics for discussion and writing.

1. In the text, King addresses the difference in understanding of the term "extremist" between the white clergymen and himself. From this example, how do you think such definitions may affect King's argument?

Extensive Reading 3

2. In his writing, King uses many metaphorical expressions, such as "the dangerously structured dam" (Para. 2), "like a boil" (Para. 2), and "quicksand of racial injustice" (Para. 4). What do you think of the effectiveness of these metaphorical comparisons in arguments? Are they good evidence to support claims?

3. King's whole letter is devoted to refuting the criticism of him and his actions from the clergymen, as can be seen from this excerpt. Why do you think King and his people should put so much weight on how other people (particularly whites) see them and on winning their support when they are struggling for their own rights?

Text B   How Food Influencers Affect What We Eat

Preparatory Work

Activity 1 Sharing of Food Pictures

Have you decided what to eat for your next meal, or this weekend? How do you usually choose the food or the restaurant? Do you often share pictures of food? Why or why not? How do you view this fashion of sharing food pictures on social media?

Credit: Jeffrey Greenberg/Getty Images; source: https://www.bbc.com/future/article/20211206-does-seeing-food-on-social-media-make-us-eat-more

How do you usually choose food or a restaurant?
Do you often share pictures of food? Why or why not?

Unit 6 Key Elements of Arguments: Claim

(continued)

How do you view this fashion of sharing food pictures on social media?

Activity 2 A Self-evaluation

Are you a person who is easily influenced by others?

Do you think being easily influenced is a positive trait? If yes, think of the possible demerits of it. If no, think of the possible merits of it.

Are you an easily influenced person? What other words you would use to describe yourself?	
Do you think being easily influenced is a positive trait? What may be the reasons for the counterargument?	

Reading the Text

In the time when our food decision is no longer made solely out of our own hunger and what happens to be at hand, what other factors can exert influence on our food choice? How can they influence us?

How Food Influencers Affect What We Eat

Jessica Brown

1 Many of us are lucky enough to have some degree of choice over what we eat. When we open the fridge or browse the shelves of the local supermarket, there are a smorgasbord of options available to us. But are the decisions we make about our diet as free as we like to think? What if there was something other than our own hunger and the choices that happen to be at eye-level influencing what we eat?

2 Scroll through social media sites such as Instagram, Twitter or Facebook and you will be confronted with picture after picture of perfectly presented and utterly delicious-looking meals. While the smell and taste of food can have an undeniably powerful effect on our cravings, are endless posts of steaming snacks and

Extensive Reading 3

glistening morsels more than just a feast for our eyes?

3   Certainly, it appears we're hugely influenced by other people—especially those closest to us—when it comes to what we eat. Research has found that the closer and stronger two people's connection, the more sway they have over each other's food choices.

4   "A lot of our cues from face-to-face interactions are linked with who we're with," says Solveig Argeseanu, associate professor of global health and epidemiology at Emory University in Atlanta, Georgia, US. "It's more about the relationship and how I compare myself with that person than specific individuals. If I think the person I'm with is more attractive or popular, I'll tend to want to imitate them more."

5   This can mean these social cues generally encourage us to eat more, Argeseanu adds. Although, being around healthy eaters may encourage you to eat healthier, too, according to research.

6   Our eating habits are also influenced by what we see. Scientists say we favour "oozing" protein, a dribbling egg yolk, or bubbling mozzarella, for example.

7   "There is some evidence that, if you see pictures of food, that visual stimulation can prompt you to feel a desire to eat," says Suzanne Higgs, professor in the psychobiology of appetite at the University of Birmingham, UK. Although, she says, whether people follow through on that desire is influenced by a lot of other factors, such as what food is available at the time.

8   But social media is one place where visual and social cues meet. There is certainly evidence that if friends in your social network post regularly about particular types of food, it could lead you to copy them, for better or for worse. And research indicates that social media might be changing our relationship with food, making us think differently about what we eat.

9   "If all your friends on social media are posting pictures of themselves consuming fast food, it's going to set a norm that eating fast food is what people do," says Higgs.

10   Research suggests we're more likely to engage with photos of fast food, says Ethan Pancer, professor of marketing at Saint Mary's University in Halifax, Nova Scotia, Canada. This is particularly true of saturated fat, because it makes us feel good by releasing dopamine and stimulating pleasure centres in the brain. Humans are biologically primed to seek out calorie-dense food—an ability that helped our ancestors survive when they foraged for food.

11   "Evolutionary psychology has found that people feel happy when they simply see these foods, and thus engage with it more," he says.

12   It doesn't help that healthier foods are often seen as boring in comparison, whereas processed food is seen as "cool", says Tina Tessitore, associate professor of marketing at the Institut d'Économie Scientifique Et de Gestion (IESEG) School of Management in Lille, France. "In advertising, you see unhealthy food in social settings—people having a barbeque with friends, for example, while healthy food often focuses more

on the nutritional value. If you saw friends eating salad together, it wouldn't seem so credible," she says.

13 Scientists are becoming increasingly concerned that food-related content on social media is making us think differently about food. Social media algorithms promote content that users engage with more, so viewing more unhealthy food means seeing more of it on our social media feeds, Pancer says.

14 "With higher engagement and reach metrics for unhealthy foods, content producers may gradually shift their content to be unhealthier to stay competitive," he says. "And with more exposure to unhealthy foods, consumer perceptions of what is considered normal eating habits may skew to be unhealthier."

15 One study estimated that children and adolescents see marketing for food between 30 and 189 times per week on social media apps, with fast food and sugary drinks being the most common. But it's not just advertising placements from the food industry that are responsible—we're all capable of influencing people online.

16 "When we think of advertising, we think of industry trying push a product, but influencers can work in the same way," says Patricia Cavazos, professor of psychiatry at Washington University School of Medicine, in St. Louis, Missouri, US. "Content on social media from peers is very influential, in terms of impacting what we feel is relevant and appealing, and social norms of how to behave."

Credit: Don Arnold/Getty Images; source: https://www.bbc.com/future/article/20211206-does-seeing-food-on-social-media-make-us-eat-more

17 It starts to get risky, Cavazo says, if the content people see perpetuates an unhealthy body image, for example.

18 "Some of us are less influenced by content, but for others who are already at risk and may have symptoms of eating disorders, having more content that normalises unhealthy eating patterns could trigger someone to move towards unhealthy behaviours."

19 But while studies have found that social media can make us think differently about food, and that we typically engage more with content featuring unhealthy food, it's uncertain yet whether this actually translates to our changes in our behaviour in daily life.

20 "If I'm scrolling through Instagram, looking at photos of tasty food, whether I seek out the food I'm prompted to seek out depends on how hungry I am, and whether it's appropriate in that moment," says Higgs.

21 And when we do eat, we're influenced by more than what we've seen online, she adds.

22 "Research would suggest that, when making a decision about what and how much to eat, we're combining different pieces of information," says Higgs. "Momentary influences come together in ways we

don't understand very well."

23   Research has found that these influences can include level of nutritional knowledge, body ideals, cooking skills and cost.

24   And while researchers can relatively easily isolate possible influences on social media to see how it affects our diets, there's much more going on in real life that these studies can't look at, Higgs says.

25   "It's possible for some people in certain situations that social media could be the predominant factor that influences their behaviour, but it's only one factor," she adds.

26   The amount of influence social media has on us also varies by individual, says Melissa Atkinson, a lecturer in psychology, at the University of Bath, UK.

27   "There's a lot of individual difference in terms of how we respond to social media images, in terms of our own biological and psychological processes," she says. Some people have a higher reward response to food cues, for example, where the brain sends out pleasure signals after seeing certain foods, Atkinson says. These people are more likely to respond to food cues no matter where they see them.

28   But even without definitive answers, researchers are looking at ways to make social media influence our diets in positive ways.

29   Tessitore, for example, has found a way to make healthier food seem more exciting on social media. She created two Twitter pages that were identical apart from one detail—one had 23 followers, while the other had more than 400,000.

30   Both accounts published the same tweet about eating healthy food. She showed participants to one of the two accounts, and when asked afterwards how likely they were to eat a salad, those who saw the account with more followers were more inclined to want to eat a salad.

31   This is because the more we assume someone has influence, the more likely we are to be influenced by them ourselves, Tessitore says.

Credit: Fiona Goodall/Getty Images; source:
https://www.bbc.com/future/article/20211206-does-seeing-food-on-social-media-make-us-eat-more

³² While the findings don't reflect reality, where we're typically exposed to multiple streams of information, images and tweets, we'd still notice and process how many followers a Twitter account has, Tessitore says, so it's likely to have the same effect.

³³ But at the moment, we're a long way from being able to nudge people towards healthier diets with posts about salads and steering people away from the powerful pictures of oozing protein.

³⁴ "We're fighting years of evolution here," says Pancer. "There's a reason we've evolved to look for calorie-dense food in food-scarce environments. But eating what feels good is misfiring—we now need to find ways to recalibrate this."

³⁵ Pancer has found in his research that, as soon as we demystify why seeing photos of burgers and chips feels good, the feel-good effect goes away. In other words—if we understand that we're biologically programmed to feel good when we see photos of burgers, perhaps we can become less prone to being influenced by it.

³⁶ In one study, he and his team asked participants to watch one of two videos, one with calorie-light and one with calorie-dense foods. Those who watched more calorie-dense foods felt more positive afterwards.

³⁷ In the second part of the study, he told participants that their feelings weren't based on the food they were about to see, but on a low-frequency, mood-boosting sound that was being played, one which wasn't detectable to humans, while a second group had no influence.

³⁸ Those who were told about the sound were no more likely to report that they'd engage with the video on social media after watching the video of calorie-dense food.

³⁹ But ultimately, when we click off social media and go back into real life, the many influences on what and how we eat are still much stronger, experts say.

⁴⁰ "I expect that food cues are stronger in person," says Argeseanu. "We're not engaging in the same way when scrolling through photos, and we're not engaging for long. Also, some research shows that if we're scrolling through lots of photos, we start to tune them out—we start to feel something that feels like satiety, as if we've eaten them all."

⁴¹ At least if you do choose to only enjoy these feasts over Instagram, it won't leave you needing to loosen your belt.

(Source: bbc.com, December 7, 2021.)

Remembering and Understanding

Activity 1 Answer the Questions in the Text

At the beginning of the text, the author raises some questions without giving her answers directly. Try to

Extensive Reading 3

answer the following questions based on your personal opinion and your understanding of the text.

Questions	My personal answer	The answer intended by the author
But are the decisions we make about our diet as free as we like to think? (Para. 1) If not, what are we influenced by?		
What if there was something other than our own hunger and the choices that happen to be at eye-level influencing what we eat? (Para. 1) What would this "something" include?		
While the smell and taste of food can have an undeniably powerful effect on our cravings, are endless posts of steaming snacks and glistening morsels more than just a feast for our eyes? (Para. 2) If yes, what else are they?		

Activity 2 Identify and Synthesize Information

In the text, the author explains in detail how our food choice decisions are influenced and the researchers' concern. How does the author develop her ideas? Answer the questions, fill in the blanks, and mark your choices in the chart below, based on the content of the text.

Introduction (Paras. _____)	What is the central idea in these paragraphs?

Unit 6 Key Elements of Arguments: Claim

(continued)

Two factors that influence our food choices (Paras. _____)	When it comes to what we eat, we are easily influenced by _____, especially those _____, and by _____, especially _____. These two factors <u>are/are not</u> the only factors for food decisions.
Effect of social media (Paras. _____)	Social media combines _____, and might change _____, making us _____. ❖ Why do we love fast food? ❖ What will food-related content on social media probably make us think about food?
Other factors and the possible consequences (Paras. _____)	Besides _____ from the food industry and content on _____, many other factors can also affect our behaviour regarding our diets, like _____. Although the effect of social media varies _____, the result may be _____ since the content that _____ unhealthy eating patterns could encourage _____ behaviours.
Researchers' efforts in seeking change to the positive (Paras. _____)	On realizing the heavy influence that social media has on our diets, researchers are looking at ways to _____. Tessitore's way is to _____ because _____. Pancer's research finds that _____.
Complexity of the issue (Paras. _____)	However influential _____ is, the issue is much more complicated because the influences in _____ are still much stronger. Food cues are stronger _____, according to Argeseanu, since viewing too many food pictures may give you sense of _____.

Reasoning and Analyzing

Activity 1 Analyze the Quotes

The author quotes heavily in this article and provides detailed information about the identity of each source. What do you think is the effect of the detailed information to introduce each source?

Extensive Reading 3

Quoting is often applied by arguers to support their points. Let's pick out some pieces from the text and briefly analyze them. What idea does the author intend to support with each quote? Fill in the blanks in the following table with your analysis.

Source	Solveig Argeseanu, associate professor of global health and epidemiology at Emory University in Atlanta, Georgia, US
Quote	"We're not engaging in the same way when scrolling through photos, and we're not engaging for long. Also, some research shows that if we're scrolling through lots of photos, we start to tune them out—we start to feel something that feels like satiety, as if we've eaten them all." (Para. 40)
Idea	
Source	Suzanne Higgs, professor in the psychobiology of appetite at the University of Birmingham, UK
Quote	"There is some evidence that, if you see pictures of food, that visual stimulation can prompt you to feel a desire to eat…" (Para. 7)
Idea	
Source	Ethan Pancer, professor of marketing at Saint Mary's University in Halifax, Nova Scotia, Canada
Quote	"We're fighting years of evolution here," says Pancer. "There's a reason we've evolved to look for calorie-dense food in food-scarce environments. But eating what feels good is misfiring—we now need to find ways to recalibrate this." (Para. 34)
Idea	

(continued)

Source	Tina Tessitore, associate professor of marketing at the Institut d'Économie Scientifique Et de Gestion (IESEG) School of Management in Lille, France
Quote	"In advertising, you see unhealthy food in social settings—people having a barbeque with friends, for example, while healthy food often focuses more on the nutritional value. If you saw friends eating salad together, it wouldn't seem so credible…" (Para. 12)
Idea	
Source	Patricia Cavazos, professor of psychiatry at Washington University School of Medicine, in St. Louis, Missouri, US
Quote	"Some of us are less influenced by content, but for others who are already at risk and may have symptoms of eating disorders, having more content that normalises unhealthy eating patterns could trigger someone to move towards unhealthy behaviours." (Para. 18)
Idea	
Source	Melissa Atkinson, a lecturer in psychology, at the University of Bath, UK
Quote	Some people have a higher reward response to food cues, for example, where the brain sends out pleasure signals after seeing certain foods, Atkinson says. These people are more likely to respond to food cues no matter where they see them. (Para. 27)
Idea	

Activity 2 What Kind of Claim Is It?

What is the claim of this text? What kind of claim is it? Can it be classified neatly into any one group, or is it a combination of types?

What is the claim?

Extensive Reading 3

What kind of claim is it?

 Reflecting and Creating

Activity 1 Topics for Discussion and Writing

1. The author refers again and again to "research" and "study" throughout the whole text. Note these examples: "Research has found..." in Para. 3, "according to research" in Para. 5, "research indicates..." in Para. 8, "One study estimated..." in Para. 15, "studies have found..." in Para. 19, and those in Paras. 22, 23, 40, to name a few. For these research efforts and studies, she does not give any details. However, at the end of the text, she describes the research procedure of Pancer's study. What do you think are the merits and demerits of these two techniques: merely referring to a study and giving a detailed description? Do you think the author uses these two ways appropriately in the text? How should we use them in our own writing?

2. In the text, the author mainly focuses on the influence of social media on our food choices. However, she refers many times to other factors that may affect our diets and acknowledges the complexity of the issue. Do you think it's necessary to mention them? Did it strengthen her argument or weaken it? What may have been the author's purpose in doing so?

3. The text is based on a large amount of quoted material from researchers and professionals. Quotes carry their opinions on this issue; does this mean that this text is mainly based on subjective judgments? How do you view the effectiveness of using quotations in arguments?

Activity 2 To Be a Food Influencer

Suppose your friend, a girl from another province, will come to see you next month. She has never visited your city, so you want to entertain her with local food. Based on your understanding of the text, how would you decide which dishes or restaurants to recommend to her? How do you plan to influence her into trying some food that you know would be hard for her to accept?

My plan for food choices	My plan for influencing her

Unit 6 Key Elements of Arguments: Claim

Summary

💡 Self-reflection

Fill out the checklist.

Area	Yes / No?	Notes / Comment
I know the importance of an early and direct claim.		
I know what claims of fact are.		
I know what claims of value are.		
I know what claims of policy are.		
I know the complexity of claims in real arguments.		
I have learned more about Martin Luther King Jr. and the American civil rights movement.		
I have gotten a deeper understanding of how we are influenced on social media, especially about food choices.		

Value Cultivation

Activity 1 Ethnic Unity

China is a country of, altogether, 56 ethnic groups. How to unite these ethnic groups? What is the key to fostering the unity and harmonious coexistence of all ethnic groups? Write your understanding in the box below and share it with your classmates.

My understanding:

Extensive Reading 3

Activity 2 Being a Reasonable and Upright Influencer

Posting on social media is becoming increasingly popular nowadays in the world. People often record or broadcast what they do or eat or experience to share with friends or strangers. Wanting to talk about one's experiences is natural and understandable, but to become internet celebrities, some people go to extremes. Take food broadcasting, for example. Chinese food culture has a long history and has always emphasized reverence and respect for food. The original intention of "food broadcasting" is to recommend high-quality food and dishes and share the joy of tasting them, or to tell the history and stories behind them. However, many food broadcasters have shifted their focus to eating and drinking strange things or to excessive eating and drinking, which is not only harmful to health but also reflects a distorted view of food and values.

There is nothing wrong with the desire to be an influencer; the point is—How should one do this? Think about the following questions and share your opinions in class.

❖ What problems have you observed about cyber influencers and live broadcasting?

❖ How harmful are they?

❖ How can an influencer be reasonable and upright in this modern world?

❖ What other efforts are needed to build a healthy online environment?

Unit 6 Key Elements of Arguments: Claim

 Further Reading

1. "Heighten a Sense of Chinese Identity (September 27, 2019)" by Xi Jinping in *Xi Jinping: The Governance of China III*
2. *Uncle Tom's Cabin* by Harriet Beecher Stowe
3. *Shark's Fin and Sichuan Pepper* by Fuchsia Dunlop

Unit 7
Key Elements of Arguments: Support

Extensive Reading 3

Mastering Critical Reading

To determine whether or how much to accept an argument, critical readers must examine how well the claim is supported by evidence, which includes various kinds of information that the arguer uses to try to persuade readers that the claim is true or acceptable. The central message in an argument may be consistent with an audience's intuition or personal observation of the world, but a critical reader will always keep in mind that acceptable claims must be solidly grounded. In this sense, understanding the frequently used types of evidence and learning how to evaluate them become essential in critical reading.

■ **Research and Experiment**

Research is work that involves studying something to try to discover facts about it. Experimentation is deliberately designed testing, often quite complex in technology, to yield particular observations or to find out what the result will be in particular conditions. These two means are often resorted to when the issue is quite complicated or scientific. As they are usually carried out by academic or professional institutions or teams, with the help of laboratory instruments or prior theoretical results, people naturally attach more weight and credibility to the results of research and experiments.

However, not everything presented as research or experiments is surely believable. Critical readers will also evaluate the reliability of this type of evidence by asking questions:

Evaluation of research and experiment
❖ Who performed the research or experiment? Are they credible?
❖ Is the research or experiment reasonably designed and appropriately carried out?
❖ Is the result of the research or experiment properly used in the argument?
❖ Is the research or experiment sponsored by the organization that will likely exert influence on the result?

■ **Example**

Examples are especially common in arguments as they can support claims and, at the same time, enliven the writing to render the reasoning more easily understood and thus better received. Examples can be drawn from real-life events, and these are the most powerful kind of examples to support claims since real facts cannot be just brushed off or erased.

Besides using real-life events, writers sometimes also suppose a situation and design an example. These invented instances are clear in illustrating and highlighting the point under discussion because they can have all the other variables controlled or hidden. However, purely artificial cases cannot be used as evidence supporting an inference because the reality and truthfulness of the designed situation cannot be assured in real life. Sometimes, the invented case may be too fanciful. So, in reading examples, we can check their weight by asking questions like these:

Evaluation of examples
❖ Are the examples facts or invented cases?
❖ Even if an example is factual, is it taken out of context when used here?
❖ Are the examples relevant to the claim they are supposed to support?
❖ Are the examples sufficient to reach a conclusion?
❖ Are the examples representative?
❖ Are the examples up to date?

■ **Statistics**

Statistics present information in numbers, and they are especially effective in comparing different groups in numerical form and showing the distribution of sub-classes in a whole group. Statistical information often falls into two main kinds: graphic and numerical. Generally, graphic information, like graphs, charts, and tables, is more eye-catching and impressive. However, numerical expressions are better integrated into the whole writing.

Since statistics usually do not come from nothing but often are the result of research or studies, people tend to be too optimistic in receiving such evidence. Actually, it is very easy to misuse statistics, unintentionally or not, and very difficult to be sure that they are properly collected in the first place. Therefore, it is important to be sensitive to the sources and reliability of the statistics and to develop a healthy skepticism when reading statistics. Besides that, the proper interpretation and use of statistics are equally important. Can we take a higher proportion of high-score students in a certain class as proof for the conclusion that the teaching in that class is better? Which is more appropriate to show the performance of students in a class in general: the average score or the median score? Accordingly, we should not attach blind credibility to statistics in arguments. Instead, we can ask questions like:

Evaluation of statistics
❖ What is the source of the statistics? Do they originate from a disinterested and trustworthy source?
❖ Do the statistics point to a comparison between comparable things?
❖ Is the statistical evidence recent enough if necessary in the discussion?
❖ Is it appropriate to use such statistics in the current discussion?
❖ Are the statistics open to other equally plausible interpretations?

Extensive Reading 3

Factual evidence, like research results, examples, and statistics, are very powerful in supporting claims as they can be verified and their existence simply cannot be denied. Nevertheless, very often, personal opinions can also serve as evidence, especially when the testimony comes from authoritative sources.

■ **Authoritative Testimony**

This type of evidence is a statement or quote from authorities giving their opinion on a certain topic. Authorities are generally regarded as more reliable than the average person because they are more knowledgeable in their fields or are better informed with more access to relevant information. The value of the testimony depends heavily on the trustworthiness of the source and the relevance of the content. A scientist in physics may not be authoritative in the study of agriculture, and a quote from several centuries ago may not be appropriate to support the latest development in that field. When reading authoritative testimony, we can ask the following questions to decide on its credibility:

Evaluation of authoritative testimony
❖ Is the authority, however famous, really authoritative enough on the issue?
❖ Is the authority unbiased and trustworthy?
❖ Is the testimony current enough if necessary to support the claim?
❖ Is the testimony related closely to the claim?
❖ Is the testimony really necessary in the argument?

 What if authorities disagree?

■ **Appeal to Values**

Some arguments may be difficult to support with factual evidence, like arguments in aesthetic fields or about morality. In these cases, writers may rely heavily on an appeal to values, attempting to arouse specific feelings or acknowledgment of certain values from readers, such as freedom, equality, patriotism, honor, loyalty, justice, duty, or responsibility. However, such appeals are not assured of acceptance from readers because the differences among readers in age, sex, race, religion, personality, social status, culture background, and so on make value systems vary greatly from person to person. Moreover, value systems also change over time. Thus, for an appeal to values, we can evaluate the appropriateness of it by asking:

Evaluation of appeal to values
❖ Are the values clearly explained and illustrated?
❖ Is the appeal to such values relevant to the claim?

Unit 7 Key Elements of Arguments: Support

(continued)

❖ Are the values likely to be accepted by the target audience?

❖ Can the appeal to such values support the claim?

Text A — Are Women Really More Talkative Than Men?

Preparatory Work

Activity 1 Detect Gender Stereotypes

People tend to put men and women into established frameworks and regard them as so different that they are even like beings from different planets. Gender stereotypes treat men and women as categories, not individual people who have their own personalities, hopes, and dreams that make them who they are. Such stereotyping is, of course, unfair. To get beyond gender stereotypes, we need to first discover what they are. Work in small groups and try to trace the stereotypical life of a female or a male in your culture.

	What life is like for ...
♀	Example: She liked dolls and pink dresses when she was a kid.
♂	

Activity 2 Who Is More Talkative?

Do you believe that women are more talkative than men? Who talks more in your family? Do you think women (or men) are more talkative for biological reasons?

How would you define talkativeness?

Do you like talkative people? Why or why not?

153

Extensive Reading 3

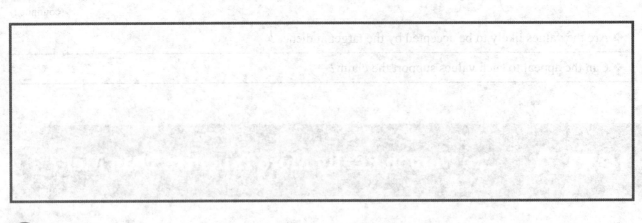

Reading the Text

Abstract: Women are generally assumed to be more talkative than men. Data were analyzed from 396 participants who wore a voice recorder that sampled ambient sounds for several days. Participants' daily word use was extrapolated from the number of recorded words. Women and men both spoke about 16,000 words per day.

Are Women Really More Talkative Than Men?

Matthias R. Mehl, Simine Vazire, Nairán Ramírez-Esparza,
Richard B. Slatcher, James W. Pennebaker[1]

[1] Sex differences in conversational behavior have long been a topic of public and scientific interest (*1, 2*). The stereotype of female talkativeness is deeply engrained in Western folklore and often considered a scientific fact. In the first printing of her book, neuropsychiatrist Brizendine[2] reported, "A woman uses about 20,000 words per day while a man uses about 7,000" (*3*). These numbers have since circulated throughout television, radio, and print media (e.g., CBS, CNN, National Public Radio, *Newsweek*, the *New York Times*, and the *Washington Post*). Indeed, the 20,000-versus-7000 word estimates appear to have achieved the status of a cultural myth in that comparable differences have been cited in the media for the past 15 years (*4*).

[2] In reality, no study has systematically recorded the natural conversations of large groups of people for extended periods of time. Consequently, there has not been the necessary data for reliably estimating differences in daily word usage among women and men (*5*). Extrapolating from a reanalysis of tape-recorded daily conversations from 153 participants from the British National Corpus (*6*), Liberman[3] recently estimated that women speak 8805 words and men 6073 words per day. However, he acknowledged that these estimates may be problematic because no information was available regarding when participants decided to turn off their manual tape recorders (*4*).

[3] Over the past 8 years, we have developed a method for recording natural language using the

electronically activated recorder (EAR) (7). The EAR is a digital voice recorder that unobtrusively tracks people's real-world moment-to-moment interactions. It operates by periodically recording snippets of ambient sounds, including conversations, while participants go about their daily lives. Because of the covert digital recording, it is impossible for participants to control or even to sense when the EAR is on or off. For the purpose of this study, the EAR can be used to track naturally spoken words and to estimate how many words women and men use over the course of a day.

4 In the default paradigm, participants wear the EAR for several days during their waking hours. The device is programmed to record for 30s every 12.5 min. All captured words spoken by the participant are transcribed. The number of spoken words per day can then be estimated by extrapolating from a simple word count, the number of sampled sound files, and the recording time per sound file.

5 We addressed the question about sex differences in daily word use with data from six samples based on 396 participants (210 women and 186 men) that were conducted between 1998 and 2004. Five of the samples were composed of university students in the United States, and the sixth, university students in Mexico. Table 1 provides background information on the samples along with estimates for the number of words that female and male participants spoke per day (8).

6 The data suggest that women spoke on average 16,215 (SD = 7301) words and men 15,669 (SD = 8633) words over an assumed period of, on average, 17 waking hours. Expressed in a common effect-size metric (Cohen's d = 0.07), this sex difference in daily word use (546 words) is equal to only 7% of the standardized variability among women and men. Further, the difference does not meet conventional thresholds for statistical significance (P = 0.248, one-sided test). Thus, the data fail to reveal a reliable sex difference in daily word use. Women and men both use on average about 16,000 words per day, with very large individual differences around this mean.

Table 1. Estimated number of words spoken per day for female and male study participants across six samples. N = 396. Year refers to the year when the data collection started; duration refers to the approximate number of days participants wore the EAR; the weighted average weighs the respective sample group mean by the sample size of the group.

Sample	Year	Location	Duration	Age range (years)	Sample size (N)		Estimated average number (SD) of words spoken per day	
					Women	Men	Women	Men
1	2004	USA	7 days	18–29	56	56	18,443 (7460)	16,576 (7871)
2	2003	USA	4 days	17–23	42	37	14,297 (6441)	14,060 (9065)
3	2003	Mexico	4 days	17–25	31	20	14,704 (6215)	15,022 (7864)
4	2001	USA	2 days	17–22	47	49	16,177 (7520)	16,569 (9108)
5	2001	USA	10 days	18–26	7	4	15,761 (8985)	24,051 (10,211)
6	1998	USA	4 days	17–23	27	20	16,496 (7914)	12,867 (8343)
				Weighted average			16,215 (7301)	15,669 (8633)

7 A potential limitation of our analysis is that all participants were university students. The resulting homogeneity in the samples with regard to sociodemographic characteristics may have affected our

estimates of daily word usage. However, none of the samples provided support for the idea that women have substantially larger lexical budgets than men. Further, to the extent that sex differences in daily word use are assumed to be biologically based, evolved adaptations (3), they should be detectable among university students as much as in more diverse samples. We therefore conclude, on the basis of available empirical evidence, that the widespread and highly publicized stereotype about female talkativeness is unfounded.

References and Notes

(1) R. Lakoff, *Language and Woman's Place* (Harper, New York, 1975).

(2) L. Litosseliti, *Gender and Language: Theory and Practice* (Arnold, London, 2006).

(3) L. Brizendine, *The Female Brain* (Morgan Road, New York, 2006).

(4) M. Liberman, *Sex-Linked Lexical Budgets*, http://itre.cis.upenn.edu/~myl/languagelog/archives/003420.html (first accessed 12 December 2006).

(5) D. James, J. Drakich, in *Gender and Conversational Interaction*, D. Tannen, Ed. (Oxford Univ. Press, New York, 1993), pp. 281—313.

(6) P. Rayson, G. Leech, M. Hodges, *Int. J. Corpus Linguist.* 2, 133 (1997).

(7) M. R. Mehl, J. W. Pennebaker, M. Crow, J. Dabbs, J. Price, *Behav. Res. Methods Instrum. Comput.* 33, 517 (2001).

(8) Details on methods and analysis are available on *Science* Online.

(9) This research was supported by a grant from the National Institute of Mental Health (MH 52391). We thank V. Dominguez, J. Greenberg, S. Holleran, C. Mehl, M. Peterson, and T. Schmader for their valuable feedback.

(Source: This article, with "References and Notes" and the preceding "Abstract", was published in *Science*, VOL. 317, July 6, 2007.)

Notes

1. **Matthias R. Mehl** is from the Department of Psychology, University of Arizona, Tucson; **Simine Vazire** from the Department of Psychology, Washington University, St. Louis, USA.; and **Nairán Ramírez-Esparza**, **Richard B. Slatcher**, and **James W. Pennebaker** from the Department of Psychology, University of Texas, USA.

2. **Louann Brizendine** is a professor of psychiatry at University of California at San Francisco. She founded the Women's Mood and Hormone Clinic at UCSF. Of her many writings, the *New York Times* bestseller *The Female Brain* has been translated into more than thirty languages.

3. **Mark Liberman** is the director of the Linguistic Data Consortium and is a professor of linguistics in the

Department of Linguistics and professor in the Department of Computer and Information Science at the University of Pennsylvania.

 Remembering and Understanding

Activity 1 Different Studies

In the article, besides giving their own research and conclusions, the authors introduce two previous studies. Collect information on these three research efforts.

Research from ...	Number of words per woman per day	Number of words per man per day	(Possible) Conclusion	Limitation
Brizendine				
Liberman				
Matthias R. Mehl et al.				

Activity 2 Identify Research Procedures

The authors explain in detail how they carried out their research in the article. Collect information on their research and fill in the following blanks.

Research purpose	
Research question	
Subjects	
Device	
Method	
Finding	

Extensive Reading 3

(continued)

Research conclusion	
Research limitation	

Reasoning and Analyzing

Answer the following questions.

1. What does the title imply?
   _____
   _____

2. Why do the authors research this topic?
   _____
   _____

3. What would the authors possibly think of the reliability of the previous two studies? What are the clues from the text?
   _____
   _____

4. Why do Brizendine's estimates appear to be a cultural myth?
   _____
   _____

5. According to the article, what are the features of reliable research on this topic?
   _____
   _____

6. The article gives details of Liberman's research. Compared with the authors' research, what other limitations of Liberman's research can you identify?
   _____
   _____

7. In the last paragraph, the authors point out that, "The resulting homogeneity in the samples with regard to sociodemographic characteristics may have affected our estimates of daily word usage." How would it possibly affect their estimates?
   _____
   _____

8. Despite the homogeneity in the samples, the authors finally conclude that female talkativeness is unfounded. Why won't this limitation affect their conclusion? What is the logic behind this reasoning?
   _____
   _____

9. What other limitations can you find about the authors' research?
   _____
   _____

Reflecting and Creating

Activity 1 Topics for Discussion and Writing

1. As the authors say at the beginning of the article, "The stereotype of female talkativeness is deeply engrained in Western folklore and often considered a scientific fact." Then, can this single research project by the authors be convincing that "the widespread and highly publicized stereotype about female talkativeness is unfounded"? If yes, what are the strengths of their research that make it so powerful? If no, what other studies are needed to verify or refute this stereotype?

2. When the article refers to the other two estimates, it presents them differently. It quotes the numbers from Brizendine without releasing any information about how they were obtained. In contrast, for Liberman's numbers, it gives some details about the research, like the size of the sample, and even includes Liberman's acknowledgment of the main problem with his study. What do you think of these two ways of delivering information? How might they affect readers?

3. This article takes a scientific perspective on gender stereotypes about talkativeness. This topic surely can be argued in other ways, like giving the claim directly and then supporting it with examples and quotes from authorities. What are the merits and demerits of these two approaches to arguing? Which do you think is more appropriate for this topic?

Activity 2 Replicate the Experiment

   The authors have told us in detail how they carried out this experiment. Now, let's try to replicate the experiment to see whether your results are in line with theirs. Try to collect as many subjects as possible. Make full use of your digital devices. You may make some adjustments to the experiment to increase its operability; for example, you might record the utterances of subjects in certain period of the day. Collect the data after some time and analyze it. Remember to note down your findings and give your conclusion. Are they consistent with the article's findings and conclusion?

   Design your experiment carefully before you start.

Extensive Reading 3

Our research purpose	
Subjects	
Device	
Method	
Finding	
Our research conclusion	
Our research limitation	

Text B Who Does the Talking Here?

Preparatory Work

Activity 1 How She Speaks, How He Speaks

Besides the stereotype of women's talkativeness, the *ways* that women and men speak are alleged to be different, too. Have you noticed any features in your own speaking? What kind of words do you like to use? Nouns, adjectives, verbs, or any other? What kind of adjectives do you often use? What kind of sentence or intonation do you use more frequently? Are there any other notable features in your way of speaking or communicating? Write them down and compare them with those of a a female classmate and a male classmate. Is there any difference? If yes, do you think this difference possibly results from gender difference?

How I Speak	How She Speaks	How He Speaks

160

Possible reasons for the difference (If there is any)

Activity 2 You Are What You Say

More readily accepted than gender stereotypes may be the notion that what you say and how you speak can reveal your personality to a certain extent. Read the following excerpt and try to make out what kind of person the speaker may be.

"Oh! My dear Mr. Bennet," as she entered the room, "we have had a most delightful evening, a most excellent ball. I wish you had been there. Jane was so admired, nothing could be like it. Everybody said how well she looked; and Mr. Bingley thought her quite beautiful, and danced with her twice. Only think of that my dear; he actually danced with her twice; and she was the only creature in the room that he asked a second time. First of all, he asked Miss Lucas. I was so vexed to see him stand up with her; but, however, he did not admire her at all: indeed, nobody can, you know; and he seemed quite struck with Jane as she was going down the dance. So, he enquired who she was, and got introduced, and asked her for the two next. Then, the two third he danced with Miss King, and the two fourth with Maria Lucas, and the two fifth with Jane again, and the two sixth with Lizzy, and the Boulanger—"

What kind of person the speaker may be	Clues from the excerpt

Reading the Text

> When a scientific study claims to break the stereotypical image of women's talkativeness by counting utterances, Dr. Tannen challenges that conclusion with a question—Can we learn who talks more by counting words?

Who Does the Talking Here?

Deborah Tannen[1]

1. It's no surprise that a one-page article published this month in the journal *Science* inspired innumerable newspaper columns and articles. The study, by Matthias Mehl and four colleagues, claims to lay to rest, once and for all, the stereotype that women talk more than men, by proving—scientifically—that women and men talk equally.

2. The notion that women talk more was reinforced last year when Louann Brizendine's "The Female Brain" cited the finding that women utter, on average, 20,000 words a day, men 7,000. (Brizendine later disavowed the statistic, as there was no study to back it up.) Mehl and his colleagues outfitted 396 college students with devices that recorded their speech. The female subjects spoke an average of 16,215 words a day, the men 15,669. The difference is insignificant. Case closed.

3. Or is it? Can we learn who talks more by counting words? No, according to a forthcoming article surveying 70 studies of gender differences in talkativeness. (Imagine—70 studies published in scientific journals, and we're still asking the question.) In their survey, Campbell Leaper and Melanie Ayres found that counting words yielded no consistent differences, though number of words per speaking turn did. (Men, on average, used more.)

4. This doesn't surprise me. In my own research on gender and language, I quickly surmised that to understand who talks more, you have to ask: What's the situation? What are the speakers using words for?

5. The following experience conveys the importance of situation. I was addressing a small group in a suburban Virginia living room. One man stood out because he talked a lot, while his wife, who was sitting beside him, said nothing at all. I described to the group a complaint common among women about men they live with: At the end of a day she tells him what happened, what she thought and how she felt about it. Then she asks, "How was your day?"—and is disappointed when he replies, "Fine," "Nothing much" or "Same old rat race".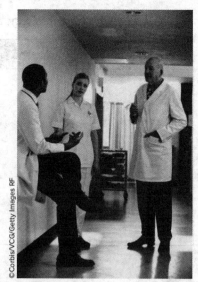

Who is the most passive figure in this group?

6. The loquacious man spoke up. "You're right," he said. Pointing to his wife, he added, "She's the talker in our family." Everyone laughed. But he explained, "It's true. When we come home, she does all the talking. If she didn't, we'd spend the evening in silence."

7. The "how was your day?" conversation typifies the kind of talk women tend to do more of: spoken to intimates and focusing on personal experience, your own or others'. I call this "rapport-talk". It contrasts with "report-talk"—giving or exchanging information about impersonal topics, which men tend to do more.

8   Studies that find men talking more are usually carried out in formal experiments or public contexts such as meetings. For example, Marjorie Swacker observed an academic conference where women presented 40 percent of the papers and were 42 percent of the audience but asked only 27 percent of the questions; their questions were, on average, also shorter by half than the men's questions. And David and Myra Sadker showed that boys talk more in mixed-sex classrooms—a context common among college students, a factor skewing the results of Mehl's new study.

9   Many men's comfort with "public talking" explains why a man who tells his wife he has nothing to report about his day might later find a funny story to tell at dinner with two other couples (leaving his wife wondering, "Why didn't he tell me first?").

10   In addition to situation, you have to consider what speakers are doing with words. Campbell and Ayres note that many studies find women doing more "affiliative speech" such as showing support, agreeing or acknowledging others' comments. Drawing on studies of children at play as well as my own research of adults talking, I often put it this way: For women and girls, talk is the glue that holds a relationship together. Their best friend is the one they tell everything to. Spending an evening at home with a spouse is when this kind of talk comes into its own. Since this situation is uncommon among college students, it's another factor skewing the new study's results.

11   Women's rapport-talk probably explains why many people think women talk more. A man wants to read the paper, his wife wants to talk; his girlfriend or sister spends hours on the phone with her friend or her mother. He concludes: Women talk more.

12   Yet Leaper and Ayres observed an overall pattern of men speaking more. That's a conclusion women often come to when men hold forth at meetings, in social groups or when delivering one-on-one lectures. All of us—women and men—tend to notice others talking more in situations where we talk less.

13   Counting may be a start—or a stop along the way—to understanding gender differences. But it's understanding when we tend to talk and what we're doing with words that yields insights we can count on.

(Source: *The Washington Post*, July 15, 2007.)

Notes

1. **Deborah Frances Tannen** (1945—) is an American academic and professor of linguistics at Georgetown University. She has written and edited many books and articles on linguistics, discourse analysis, and interpersonal communication for general audiences as well as scholarly audiences. Her book *You Just Don't Understand: Women and Men in Conversation*, published in 1990, remained on the *New York Times* Best Seller list for nearly four years (eight months at No.1) and has been translated into 31 languages.

Extensive Reading 3

 Remembering and Understanding

Activity 1 Match the Key Information and Questions

The following is a list of key information in the text and some questions about the content. Choose the information that is most related to each question and give a complete answer based on the information you choose.

List of Key Information:

A. talking as a means to hold a relationship

B. experiment of counting words

C. in formal experiments or public contexts such as meetings

D. Counting alone cannot yield reliable conclusion.

E. women and men being equally talkative

F. spoken to intimates and focusing on personal experience—your own or others'

G. when we tend to talk and what we're doing with words

Question	Key information	Complete answer
1. What is the conclusion of Mehl et al.'s study?		
2. How did Mehl and his colleagues reach this conclusion?		
3. What does the author think of Mehl et al.'s conclusion reached by counting words?		
4. Compared to those counting words, what other studies are more meaningful and significant on this issue?		
5. According to the author, in which situation will men talk more?		
6. What kind of talk do women tend to use more than men?		
7. What does talk mean to women?		

164

Unit 7 Key Elements of Arguments: Support

Reasoning and Analyzing

Answer the following questions.

1. What is the claim or thesis of the text?

2. According to your understanding of the text, how would you answer the question in the title?

3. What is the author's attitude toward Mehl et al.'s study? What clues can you make out from the text?

4. Why does the author consider the result of Mehl et al.'s study as not quite reliable? What are the problems with their study?

5. What may be the implication of the author's mentioning her "own research on gender and language" (Para. 4)?

6. In Para. 5, the author describes a common complaint from women. "At the end of a day she tells him what happened, what she thought and how she felt about it. Then she asks, 'How was your day?'—and is disappointed when he replies, 'Fine' 'Nothing much' or 'Same old rat race'." Based on your understanding of the text, how would you explain the situation?

7. According to the text, why do we tend to think the other gender talks more?

8. What are the foundations for the author's objection to Mehl et al.'s results? What kind of evidence does she give to support her claim?

Extensive Reading 3

 Reflecting and Creating

Topics for discussion and writing.

1. Both of the articles, Text A and Text B in this unit, use scientific studies to support their claims. How differently do they use scientific research? Does each article use them effectively? How can we use scientific research in our arguments?

2. Based on the content of this article, can you provide some possible explanation for the way the speaker talks in Activity 2 of Preparatory Work at the beginning of Text B? What do you think of your explanation, compared with the proposal that the speaker's personality brings that result?

3. What is the research purpose and conclusion of Mehl et al.'s study? What is the conclusion of this article? How closely are they related? Are they comparable?

Summary

 Self-reflection

Fill out the checklist.

Area	Yes / No?	Notes / Comment
I know the power of research and experiments as evidence and how to evaluate them.		
I know the distinction between real examples and hypothetical examples, and how to evaluate them as evidence.		
I know the power of statistics as evidence and how to evaluate them.		
I know the power of authoritative testimony as evidence and how to evaluate it.		
I know the power of appeal to values as evidence and how to evaluate it.		
I have obtained a deeper understanding of gender stereotypes.		

Unit 7　Key Elements of Arguments: Support

 **Value Cultivation**

As said in Text A, the stereotype of female talkativeness "is deeply engrained in Western folklore" and is presented in many proverbs, such as

- *A woman's tongue wags like a lamb's tail.*
- *Foxes are all tail, and women are all tongue.*
- *Nothing is so unnatural as a talkative man or a quiet woman.*
- *The North Sea will sooner be found wanting in water than a woman be at a loss for a word.*

Translate the above proverbs into Chinese and then find some Chinese culture proverbs or idiomatic expressions that carry gender stereotypes.

Translation of above proverbs
Chinese proverbs of gender stereotypes

Where do you think these gender differences come from? Are they biologically set? How should we view the differences between genders?

Extensive Reading 3

 Further Reading

1. *Men Are from Mars, Women Are from Venice* by John Gray
2. *You Just Don't Understand: Women and Men in Conversation* by Deborah Tannen
3. *Historic Girls* by Elbridge Streeter Brooks
4. "Emma Watson: Gender equality is your issue too" (2004), https://www.unwomen.org/en/news/stories/2014/9/emma-watson-gender-equality-is-your-issue-too

Unit 8
Key Elements of Arguments: Assumptions

Mastering Critical Reading

All arguments, whether inductive or deductive, begin with assumptions which may or may not be justified. In most cases, these assumptions are implied rather than stated, so recognizing and examining assumptions is perhaps the most crucial practical skill in critical reading.

Source: 5 Assumptions That Sabotage Your Marketing

■ **What are Assumptions?**

Assumptions are unexamined facts, ideas, or beliefs, which may be stated or unstated. An assumption in an argument is something the argument takes for granted and depends upon for its validity and in reaching its conclusion. It is accepted as true or as certain to happen, without proof. For example:

All kids are excited when they get new toys. Tim will be thrilled when he gets the new radio-controlled car we bought him.

Here, it is being assumed that Tim is a kid. However, if someone were to claim that "Tim is from Australia" was an assumption here, that claim would be incorrect. Tim does not have to be from Australia for the conclusion to be correct. Tim could be from China or Italy; the conclusion would still be fine.

■ **Explicit and Implicit Assumptions**

An explicit assumption is one stated in the argument. In the above example, "all kids are excited when they get new toys" is an explicit assumption. We assume the accuracy of this information in the argument. Implicit assumptions are not stated, but nevertheless must be true for the conclusion to be true. In the above example, "Tim is a kid" is an implicit assumption required to reach the conclusion.

■ **Recognize Implicit Assumptions**

Writers often present incomplete arguments by omitting some premises from their statements. The more

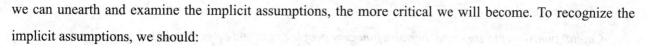

Unit 8 Key Elements of Arguments: Assumptions

we can unearth and examine the implicit assumptions, the more critical we will become. To recognize the implicit assumptions, we should:

❖ Identify the conclusion of the argument.

❖ Identify what is stated in the author's reasoning or evidence.

❖ Make the inference that connects the author's reasoning or evidence to the conclusion in a convincing way.

For example:

The school is superior to most others because its ratio of students to teachers is low.

Conclusion: This school is superior to most others.

Evidence: Its ratio of students to teachers is low.

Assumption 1 (implicit): Students in this school will get more attention.

Assumption 2 (implicit): More attention results in a better education.

■ **The Audience's Varied Assumptions Differing from the author's**

While it is common and understandable for a writer or speaker to leave certain ideas implicit because they believe them to be true and acceptable, the audience may disagree with these unspoken assumptions. The unstated information may be just some belief acquired because of conditions where the author was brought up, or it may be a well-grounded fact or well-accepted belief for a certain group of people or a certain culture but not for another. We need to always keep alert for the stated reasoning and, more importantly, the unstated. What is the implicit assumption of the following argument? Do you agree with it?

Argument	Abortion should not be permitted.
Assumption	

■ **Examine Different Types of Assumptions**

Since assumptions are unexamined facts, ideas, or beliefs, we should be attentive to them because they are sometimes incorrect or misguided. To be critical readers, we need to recognize them, bring them out into the light, and examine them by asking questions.

	Factual assumptions	Analytical assumptions	Assumptions relating to values and beliefs
Examples	Tim is a Kid.	Smoking is a serious health hazard.	Anything that kills innocent people is immoral.
How to examine	It can be measured or observed directly.	It can be defended with reason and evidence.	It is almost impossible to prove values. Either you share them, or you don't.

Extensive Reading 3

For example:

Capital punishment is immoral because innocent people might end up getting killed by the death penalty.

Even if we don't agree, the reasoning sounds complete. However, to reach the conclusion from the premise, what implicit assumption does this argument necessarily imply about things that might kill innocent people?

Conclusion: Capital punishment is immoral.

Evidence: The death penalty might kill innocent people.

Assumption (implicit): Anything that kills innocent people is immoral.

Is anything that kills innocent people immoral? Possible disagreements about this challenge the argument:

"Not necessarily. If so, we shouldn't give inoculations to babies because that kills some innocent people too."

A checklist for examining assumptions
❖ What assumptions does the writer's argument presuppose?
❖ Are these assumptions explicit or implicit?
❖ Are these assumptions important to the author's argument or only incidental?
❖ Does the author give any evidence of being aware of the hidden assumptions in the argument?
❖ Would a critic be likely to share these assumptions, or are they exactly what a critic would challenge?
❖ What sort of evidence would be relevant to supporting or rejecting these assumptions?
❖ Are you willing to grant the author's assumptions?
❖ If not, why not?

(Credit: Sylvan Barnet & Hugo Bedau, *Critical Thinking, Reading and Writing: A Brief Guide to Argument* [5th edition], Bedford/St. Martin's, Boston, 2005)

Enhancing Your Critical Reading (6)

Identify and examine the assumptions in the following arguments.

Arguments	Assumptions
1. Getting an English degree is a waste of an education because you'll never get rich from it.	
2. This building is in bad condition, and therefore the rent should be lowered.	

Unit 8 Key Elements of Arguments: Assumptions

(continued)

3. Drugs should remain illegal because they injure your health.	
4. Boxing causes injury, so this is not a sport we should encourage.	
5. Tom would never hurt anyone's feelings because he's very sensitive himself.	

Text A   The Higher Education Learning Crisis

Preparatory Work

Activity 1 Understand the Concept of Liberal Education

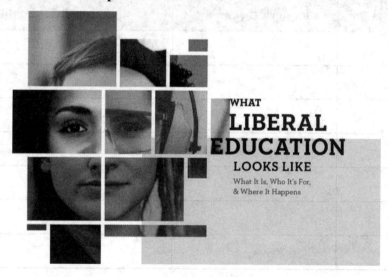

Source: What Is Liberal Education? AAC&U

Dating back to ancient Greece, with the writings of philosophers like Plato and Aristotle in the 4th century BC, liberal education has a rich and extensive history that has evolved over centuries. Get into small groups and have a discussion based on the following questions:

  ❖ What is liberal education?
  ❖ What are the primary goals of liberal education?
  ❖ What are the benefits and drawbacks of liberal education?
  ❖ What subjects or disciplines are typically included in a liberal education curriculum?

Extensive Reading 3

Activity 2 Design Your Curriculum

Source: Higher Education in Germany

The goal of higher education is to foster critical thinking, intellectual curiosity, and a well-rounded understanding of the world, preparing individuals with specific learning outcomes that are essential for work, citizenship, and life. Look into your curriculum to see what courses are truly essential to achieve the goal. Who do you think is responsible for the curriculum?

Essential courses	Irrelevant courses	Course that should be added

Reading the Text

> Despite society's expectation for education to offer avenues for students to enhance themselves and their communities, Richard H. Hersh and Richard Keeling raise concerns about a crisis in American higher education at the undergraduate level where students are failing to acquire essential learning. They urge faculty and students alike to embrace the ongoing cumulative and collective nature of higher learning while constantly aiming for higher standards of competence.

The Higher Education Learning Crisis

Richard H. Hersh and Richard Keeling[1]

Job ticket? University of Denver graduates celebrate their achievements,
and journalism students try to learn in a large classroom at the University of Missouri

1   There is a crisis in American undergraduate higher education requiring a shift away from spurious magazine rankings, unacceptable graduation rates, inequitable admissions selectivity, rising costs, and administrative and faculty inefficiency to a more fundamental problem: Students do not learn enough in college, period.

2   This higher learning crisis is not unique to the United States, although here it is more documented and publicly discussed. For the past several decades, high costs and unemployment catalyzed public demand for greater accountability and learning assessment. Many countries, unlike the United States, rely on exit exams, but only recently have researchers studied institutions' impact on learning compared to appropriate peers—how much, for example, is institutional quality a measure of learning caused by attendance at a specific institution versus entrance selectivity, what is known as the "diamonds in, diamonds out" phenomenon.

3   Other countries have emulated American universities because of prestigious worldwide rankings, but such emulation may be hollow as rankings are based on scholarship and research prowess, measured by numbers of publications and scholarly citations, not undergraduate learning. Indeed, higher education globally continues to follow a relatively passive learning tradition with full responsibility for learning placed on students. Ironically, some of the world's best teaching and learning now happens on campuses jointly run by host countries and American universities, like Yale and the National University of Singapore[2]. A new beginning allows faculty the freedom and creativity to develop more efficacious, learner-centered curricula and pedagogy.

4   Too many graduates are not prepared to think critically and creatively, speak and write cogently, solve problems, comprehend complex issues, accept accountability, take the perspective of others, or meet employer expectations. In their 2010 book *Academically Adrift: Limited Learning on College Campuses*[3], Richard Arum and Josipa Roksa provide statistical evidence that most students do not make significant gains in critical thinking, problem-solving, analytical reasoning and written communication skills while in

college—showing that the gap between what institutions promise and what they deliver has become a chasm.

5   In 2006, the Spellings Commission on the Future of Higher Education[4] scathingly labeled higher education as "risk-aversive" "self-satisfied" "unduly expensive" and "ineffective". In a landmark study, *Greater Expectations: A New Vision for Learning as a Nation Goes to College*[5], the Association of American Colleges and Universities relayed the urgency: "even as college attendance is rising, the performance of too many students is faltering." This costly failure—in the face of a seemingly inexorable precipitous rise in tuition costs and student loan burden—must be resolved to sustain political, social, economic, and scientific leadership. The claim that the American system of higher education is the "best in the world" has become an empty accolade masking inadequate quality and quantity of learning.

6   Culture off and on campus is at the heart of the matter. The United States has bastardized the bachelor's degree by turning it into a ticket to a job. Meanwhile, the academy has adopted an increasingly customer-based ethic reaping costly effects: "Professional training" has displaced the expectations and standards of a rigorous liberal education—with teaching and learning devalued, deprioritized and replaced by an emphasis on simpleminded metrics that feed magazine rankings, enrollment, winning teams, facilities, with more revenue from sideline businesses. Teaching duties are increasingly left to adjunct faculty with few incentives for tenure-track faculty to spend time with undergraduates or improve teaching. Expectations for hard work in college have fallen victim to smorgasbord-style curricula, large lecture classes, institutional needs to retain students in order to make the budget and inflated grades for minimal student effort. None of this makes for higher learning.

7   The prevailing academic culture purveys a curricular and teaching model of credit hours per course founded on the presumption that topics and skills should be packaged into one or two courses, such as freshman composition, or a series of courses in a major or minor. Each course or series, presumed to stand alone, signifies a module of learning achievement. That module—even if it comprises the requirements for a minor or major—is too often compartmentalized and disconnected from other learning during that semester. This system conveys to students and teachers alike that learning occurs best when students stack individual courses like building blocks—as if learning becomes greater as the pile grows. But that assumption is false. No mortar connects these blocks; they topple easily, and the learning is disconnected and ephemeral.

8   A renewed academic culture must embrace the *cumulative and collective* nature of higher learning. The core learning outcomes proffered by higher education—critical thinking, effective written and oral

communication, the ability to use rather than simply acquire knowledge to solve problems—are ineffectively attained in one or two required courses or random out-of-classroom learning experiences. One or two writing seminars are insufficient for producing competent writers. A required general education course in critical thinking alone cannot teach how to evaluate credibility of information and solve problems. Students do not learn qualities of effective leadership solely by serving as an elected officer of a student organization. It is not surprising, then, to hear faculty lament, "They were supposed to learn how to—before they got to my course," filling the blank in with any number of skills. Autonomy of disciplines, lack of true investment in general education, absence of faculty consensus about what students should learn across the curriculum, and weakness of academic advising undermine any sense of coherence in students' learning. The consequence—and working assumption—is that constructing coherence among individual courses and learning experiences is the student's responsibility alone.

9   Success in achieving core higher-learning outcomes requires an approach best accomplished cumulatively—requiring more instruction, practice, assessment and feedback than is now provided, or expected, within single courses or other isolated learning experiences. Learning how to think and write creatively, for example, are skills optimally learned over the span of an entire undergraduate program intentionally planned and assessed by faculty and staff across all courses and programs. Writing-across-the-curriculum initiatives are one example of the application of this idea, but the concept can also include across-the-curriculum demand for critical thinking, problem solving and ethical development.

Source: How Are We Measuring the Success of Colleges?, GatesNotes

10   This is not to suggest that such core outcomes are content free. One must think and write about something, and subject-matter expertise is a necessary, contextual condition. Offering a smorgasbord of course offerings in the name of "student interest" only serves to reify the belief that the student as customer knows best. Knowledge acquisition by itself is not sufficient; higher learning entails the ability to apply such knowledge, using it to inform one's thinking, writing or discourse. While disciplinary competence necessarily differs across courses and programs, the core work of higher learning becomes cumulative when coursework reinforces common outcomes, intentionally progressing in complexity and sophistication towards collectively

established learning goals. For example, a well-written paper in history offering a critical analysis of the causes of World War I would share standards for critical thinking and effective writing with a paper analyzing threats to biodiversity. A cumulative approach to higher learning requires that students are taught to an increasingly higher standard of competence—thus, a more integrative, stable and coherent education.

[11] Cumulative learning requires faculty to *collectively* agree on which outcomes, expectations and standards to share and endorse, reinforcing them throughout all courses. Faculty must provide timely and appropriate feedback to students. Understanding "faculty" as a collective noun responsible for outcomes involves a substantial institutional culture shift.

[12] A college education that fails to ensure that students learn is not worth the cost at any price. High cost plus poor quality equals low value. The answer is not throwing money at problems. Societies must take steps to improve the quality and quantity of learning, changing the very culture of higher education as a whole.

(Source: YaleGlobal Online, November 22, 2018.)

Notes

1. **Richard H. Hersh,** former president of Hobart and William Smith Colleges, and Trinity College, is currently a professor of Education Studies at Yale University. **Richard Keeling**, president of Keeling & Associates, a higher education consulting practice, and former vice president for Student Affairs at the University of Wisconsin, collaborated with Hersh on the book *We're Losing Our Minds: Rethinking American Higher Education* (Palgrave, 2012).

2. **Yale and the National University of Singapore** have a collaborative partnership that resulted in the establishment of Yale-NUS College, a liberal arts college located in Singapore. It was established in 2011 as a joint venture between the two universities, making it the first liberal arts college in Singapore and one of the first in Asia.

3. Published in 2011, *Academically Adrift: Limited Learning on College Campuses* by Richard Arum and Josipa Roksa, examines the current state of higher education in the United States and raises concerns about the level of learning and academic rigor in colleges and universities.

4. The nineteen-member **Spellings Commission on the Future of Higher Education** was established on September 19, 2005, aimed at examining and improving the state of higher education in the United States.

5. Published in 2002, *Greater Expectations: A New Vision for Learning as a Nation Goes to College* edited by Carol Geary Schneider and others, focuses on the urgent need to improve the quality of education at the undergraduate level in the United States.

Unit 8 Key Elements of Arguments: Assumptions

 Remembering and Understanding

Activity 1 True or False Questions

Are the following statements true or false? Make your decisions based on the text.

(   ) 1. The higher learning crisis is a global issue.

(   ) 2. Rankings of universities are based on undergraduate learning.

(   ) 3. Other countries emulate American universities because American universities excel in undergraduate learning.

(   ) 4. Most college graduates are not adequately prepared in critical thinking and problem-solving skills.

(   ) 5. The Spellings Commission criticized higher education for being too affordable.

(   ) 6. The prevailing academic culture values teaching and learning.

(   ) 7. Learning occurs best when individual courses are stacked like building blocks.

(   ) 8. Required courses in critical thinking alone are insufficient for developing problem-solving skills.

(   ) 9. Coherence in students' learning is solely their responsibility.

(   ) 10. Providing a variety of course offerings based on student interest is beneficial for higher learning.

(   ) 11. Improving the quality and quantity of learning requires throwing money at the problems.

Activity 2 Outline the Text

How do the two authors develop their ideas? Fill in the blanks with appropriate words to get a paragraph-by-paragraph outline of the text.

Outline

Para. 1   Introduction to the crisis in American (1)_____

Para. 2   The (2)_____ nature of the higher learning crisis

Para. 3   Emulation of American universities based on rankings of (3)_____

Para. 4   Gap between (4)_____ resulting in graduates ill-prepared in skill readiness

Para. 5   Reports and studies highlighting the (5)_____ to address the crisis

Para. 6   (6)_____ affecting teaching and learning

Para. 7   The (7)_____ approach to learning and its drawbacks

Para. 8   The need for a renewed academic culture that emphasizes the (8)_____ nature of higher learning

Para. 9   The importance of a cumulative approach to achieving (9)_____

Para. 10 The importance of (10)_____ expertise in core outcomes

Para. 11 The role of (11)_____ in cumulative learning

Para. 12 The need to improve the (12)_____ of learning through cultural change in higher education

Extensive Reading 3

Reasoning and Analyzing

Activity 1 Multiple-choice Questions

Choose the best answer from the four choices given based on the text.

1. Which of the following best describes the "diamonds in, diamonds out" phenomenon as mentioned in the passage?

    A. Institutions with high entrance selectivity foster better learning outcomes.

    B. Institutions with high entrance selectivity have little impact on learning outcomes.

    C. Entrance selectivity has no correlation with learning outcomes.

    D. Institutions with low entrance selectivity have better learning outcomes.

2. What does the passage suggest is a consequence of the prevailing academic culture?

    A. Increased focus on building highly specialized skills.

    B. Greater emphasis on interdisciplinary learning.

    C. Devaluation of teaching and learning in favor of other metrics.

    D. Enhanced collaboration between faculty and adjunct instructors.

3. According to the passage, which of the following is not a reason for the inadequate quality of learning in higher education?

    A. Lack of investment in general education.

    B. Autonomy of disciplines.

    C. Weakness of academic advising.

    D. Faculty consensus about what students should learn.

4. The passage argues that higher learning outcomes are best achieved through _____.

    A. isolated learning experiences within single courses

    B. a cumulative approach across a student's entire undergraduate program

    C. focusing on increasing subject-matter expertise in each course

    D. a diverse range of extracurricular activities

5. What does the passage suggest regarding the relationship between subject-matter expertise and core learning outcomes?

    A. Subject-matter expertise is unnecessary for achieving core learning outcomes.

    B. Core learning outcomes can only be attained through subject-matter expertise.

    C. Core learning outcomes are separate from subject-matter expertise.

    D. Subject-matter expertise is important but needs to be applied to achieve core learning outcomes.

6. The passage implies that successful achievement of core higher-learning outcomes requires _____.

A. greater diversity in course offerings

B. fewer required courses and more independent learning

C. more instruction, practice, and assessment across all courses and programs

D. abandoning the concept of learning outcomes altogether

Activity 2 Identify and Analyze Assumptions

Here are some arguments taken from the essay. What are the hidden assumptions in them?

Arguments	Assumptions
1. There is a crisis in American undergraduate higher education requiring a shift away from spurious magazine rankings… to a more fundamental problem: Students do not learn enough in college, period. (Para. 1)	
2. Other countries have emulated American universities because of prestigious worldwide rankings, but such emulation may be hollow as rankings are based on scholarship and research prowess, measured by numbers of publications and scholarly citations, not undergraduate learning. (Para. 3)	
3. The evidence that most students do not make significant gains in critical thinking, problem-solving, analytical reasoning and written communication skills while in college shows that the gap between what institutions promise and what they deliver has become a chasm. (Para.4)	
4. The United States has bastardized the bachelor's degree by turning it into a ticket to a job because "professional training" has displaced the expectations and standards of a rigorous liberal education. (Para. 6)	

Extensive Reading 3

(continued)

5. A renewed academic culture must embrace the cumulative and collective nature of higher learning. (Para. 8)	
6. A college education that fails to ensure that students learn is not worth the cost at any price. (Para. 12)	

 Reflecting and Creating

Topics for discussion, writing, and presentation.

1. The passage discusses the crisis in American higher education, where students are not learning enough. However, this crisis is not unique to the United States. Do you think higher education in China is undergoing this crisis? If yes, why do you think students are not learning enough in college? Exchange your views in small groups.

2. "Culture off and on campus is at the heart of the matter. The United States has bastardized the bachelor's degree by turning it into a ticket to a job." (Para. 6) How do you perceive the emphasis on job preparation in the current higher education system in China? Do you think colleges should prioritize job skills, or should they focus more on a rigorous liberal education? Write a short essay responding to the above questions.

3. "The core learning outcomes proffered by higher education—critical thinking, effective written and oral communication, the ability to use rather than simply acquire knowledge to solve problems—are ineffectively attained in one or two required courses or random out-of-classroom learning experiences." (Para. 8) Based on your own educational experience, do you feel that these core learning outcomes were effectively developed in your required courses? If not, what changes would you suggest to better incorporate these outcomes throughout a student's college education? Do some research and write a short essay responding to the above questions.

4. "A college education that fails to ensure that students learn is not worth the cost at any price."(Para. 12) How do you personally measure the value of a college education? Should institutions be held more accountable for ensuring students learn and develop necessary skills? If so, what specific measures or changes would you recommend? Discuss in small groups and present your ideas in class.

Unit 8 Key Elements of Arguments: Assumptions

Text B   What Would Plato Say About ChatGPT?

 Preparatory Work

Activity 1 Brainstorming

Achieving 100 million users within two months of being launched in late 2022 and with around one billion interactions each month, ChatGPT, an artificial intelligence chatbot developed by OpenAI, has attracted the world's attention. What do you know about ChatGPT? Brainstorm associations and fill them in the circles:

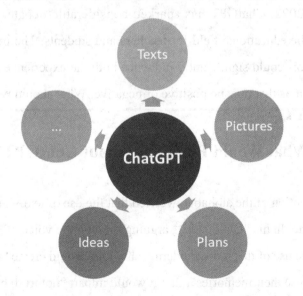

Extensive Reading 3

Activity 2 Video-watching: What Is a Flipped Classroom?

Source: 5 Flipped Classroom Activities for Elementary School Students

Have you ever experienced a flipped classroom setting? How is it different from a traditional classroom? Watch a short video about flipped classrooms and discuss the following questions based on the video.

- What is a flipped classroom like?
- How is it different from a traditional classroom?
- What are the benefits of a flipped classroom?

Reading the Text

> Since its launch in 2022, ChatGPT has sparked considerable debate, especially concerning its potential integration into the educational field for teachers and students. The implementation of ChatGPT and other generative AI tools could significantly influence both the experience and workload of educators and learners, with implications that may be positive or negative. What should we do with it?

What Would Plato Say About ChatGPT?

Zeynep Tufekci[1]

1   Plato mourned the invention of the alphabet, worried that the use of text would threaten traditional memory-based arts of rhetoric. In his "Dialogues"[2], arguing through the voice of Thamus,[3] the Egyptian king of the gods, Plato claimed the use of this more modern technology would create "forgetfulness in the learners' souls, because they will not use their memories", that it would impart "not truth but only the semblance of truth" and that those who adopt it would "appear to be omniscient and will generally know nothing", with "the show of wisdom without the reality".

2   If Plato were alive today, would he say similar things about ChatGPT?

3   ChatGPT, a conversational artificial intelligence program released recently by OpenAI, isn't just another entry in the artificial intelligence hype cycle. It's a significant advancement that can produce articles in response to open-ended questions that are comparable to good high school essays.

4   It is in high schools and even college where some of ChatGPT's most interesting and troubling aspects will become clear.

5   Essay writing is most often assigned not because the result has much value — proud parents putting good grades on the fridge aside — but because the process teaches crucial skills: researching a topic, judging claims, synthesizing knowledge and expressing it in a clear, coherent and persuasive manner. Those skills will be even more important because of advances in AI.

6   When I asked ChatGPT a range of questions — about the ethical challenges faced by journalists who work with hacked materials, the necessity of cryptocurrency regulation, the possibility of democratic backsliding in the United States — the answers were cogent, well reasoned and clear. It's also interactive: I could ask for more details or request changes.

Source: Exploring the Potential of ChatGPT in Education

7   But then, on trickier topics or more complicated concepts, ChatGPT sometimes gave highly plausible answers that were flat-out wrong—something its creators warn about in their disclaimers.

8   Unless you already knew the answer or were an expert in the field, you could be subjected to a high-quality intellectual snow job.[4]

9   You would face, as Plato predicted, "the show of wisdom without the reality."

10 All this, however, doesn't mean ChatGPT—or similar tools, because it's not the only one of its kind—can't be a useful tool in education.

11 Schools have already been dealing with the Internet's wealth of knowledge, along with its lies, misleading claims and essay mills.

12 One way has been to change how they teach. Rather than listen to a lecture in class and then go home

to research and write an essay, students listen to recorded lectures and do research at home, then write essays in class, with supervision, even collaboration with peers and teachers. This approach is called flipping the classroom.

13   In flipped classrooms, students wouldn't use ChatGPT to conjure up a whole essay. Instead, they'd use it as a tool to generate critically examined building blocks of essays. It would be similar to how students in advanced math classes are allowed to use calculators to solve complex equations without replicating tedious, previously mastered steps.

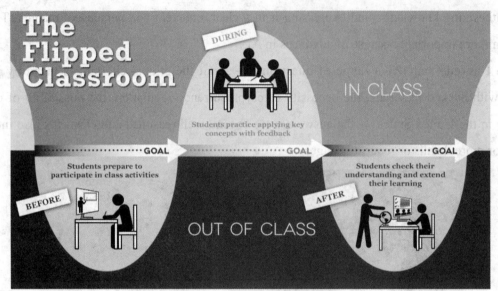

Source: What Is a Flipped Classroom?

14   Teachers could assign a complicated topic and allow students to use such tools as part of their research. Assessing the veracity and reliability of these AI-generated notes and using them to create an essay would be done in the classroom, with guidance and instruction from teachers. The goal would be to increase the quality and the complexity of the argument.

15   This would require more teachers to provide detailed feedback. Unless sufficient resources are provided equitably, adapting to conversational AI in flipped classrooms could exacerbate inequalities.

16   In schools with fewer resources, some students may end up turning in AI-produced essays without obtaining useful skills or really knowing what they have written. "Not truth but only the semblance of truth," as Plato said.

17   Some school officials may treat this as a problem of merely plagiarism detection and expand the use of draconian surveillance systems. During the pandemic, many students were forced to take tests or write essays under the gaze of an automated eye-tracking system or on a locked-down computer to prevent cheating.

18   In a fruitless arms race against conversational AI, automated plagiarism software may become supercharged, making school more punitive for monitored students. Worse, such systems will inevitably produce some false accusations, which damage trust and may even stymie the prospects of promising

students.

19 Educational approaches that treat students like enemies may teach students to hate or subvert the controls. That's not a recipe for human betterment.

20 While some students lag, advanced AI will create a demand for other advanced skills. The Nobel laureate Herbert Simon[5] noted in 1971 that as information became overwhelming, the value of our attention grew. "A wealth of information creates a poverty of attention," as he put it. Similarly, the ability to discern truth from the glut of plausible-sounding but profoundly incorrect answers will be precious.

21 Already, Stack Overflow, a widely used website where programmers ask one another coding-related questions, banned ChatGPT answers because too many of them were hard-to-spot nonsense.

Source: ChatGPT is a Paradigm Shift; Education Should Embrace It.

22 Why rely on it at all, then?

23 At a minimum, because it will soon transform many occupations. The right approach when faced with transformative technologies is to figure out how to use them for the betterment of humanity.

24 Betterment has been a goal of public education for at least the past 150 years. But while a high school diploma once led to a better job, in the past few decades, the wages of high school graduates have greatly lagged those of college graduates, fostering inequality.

25 If AI enhances the value of education for some while degrading the education of others, the promise of betterment will be broken.

26 Plato erred by thinking that memory itself is a goal, rather than a means for people to have facts at their call so they can make better analyses and arguments. The Greeks developed many techniques to memorize poems like the *Odyssey*,[6] with its more than 12,000 lines. Why bother to force this if you can have it all written down in books?

27 As Plato was wrong to fear the written word as the enemy, we would be wrong to think we should resist a process that allows us to gather information more easily.

28 As societies responded to previous technological advances, like mechanization, by eventually enacting

a public safety net, a shorter workweek and a minimum wage, we will also need policies that allow more people to live with dignity as a basic right, even if their skills have been superseded. With so much more wealth generated now, we could unleash our imagination even more, expanding free time and better working conditions for more people.

29 The way forward is not to just lament supplanted skills, as Plato did, but also to recognize that as more complex skills become essential, our society must equitably educate people to develop them. And then it always goes back to the basics. Value people as people, not just as bundles of skills.

30 And that isn't something ChatGPT can tell us how to do.

(Source: *The New York Times*, Dec. 15, 2022.)

Notes

1. **Zeynep Tufekci**, a Turkish-American sociologist and writer, gained recognition as the author of *Twitter and Tear Gas: The Power and Fragility of Networked Protest* (2017). Her insightful perspectives can be regularly found in publications such as *The Atlantic* and *The New York Times*, in addition to her newsletter called *Insight*.

2. In his ***Dialogues***, Plato presents a philosophy that has served as a guiding light for humanity across generations. Delving into our virtues and vices, as well as our pressing issues and inquiries, he eloquently illustrates how individuals can comprehend their role in the world and strive towards a life of wisdom and contentment.

3. **Thamus** is a character in Plato's dialogue *Phaedrus*. He is a mythological figure who was the king of Egypt and a renowned sage.

4. **An intellectual snow job** refers to a situation where someone uses excessive jargon, complicated language, or sophisticated arguments to impress or confuse others without actually presenting any useful information or substantial analysis. It can be seen as a form of intellectual deception or manipulation, intended to make one appear more intelligent or knowledgeable than they actually are.

5. **Herbert Simon** (1916—2001), an American economist, political scientist, and cognitive psychologist, is renowned for his expertise in decision-making and artificial intelligence. In acknowledgment of his remarkable achievements, Simon received the Turing Award in computer science in 1975 and the Nobel Prize in Economics in 1978.

6. The ***Odyssey*** by Homer is one of the most significant works in ancient Greek literature. It tells the epic tale of Odysseus's ten-year journey home after the Trojan War and explores themes of heroism, perseverance, and the challenges of the human experience.

Unit 8 Key Elements of Arguments: Assumptions

 Remembering and Understanding

Activity 1 Summarize the Text

What is the essay mainly about? Fill in the blanks with appropriate words to get a brief summary.

ChatGPT, a (1)_____ program developed by Open AI, exerts a great impact on education. Similar to Plato's concerns about undesirable effects of (2)_____, the use of ChatGPT in essay writing could lead to the (3) "_____" because it sometimes produces (4)_____ answers. However, ChatGPT can be used as a tool in (5)_____, where students generate (6)_____ that are critically examined and expanded upon under the guidance and instructions of teachers. Potential issues of (7)_____ may arise from incorporating ChatGPT into education. Therefore, there is a need for educational approaches that prioritize critical thinking and the ability to (8)_____. Ultimately, society should focus on using (9)_____ like AI for the betterment of humanity and ensure (10)_____ to education and opportunities.

Activity 2 Multiple-choice Questions

Choose the best answer from the four choices given based on the text.

1. Plato's concerns about the invention of the alphabet were that _____.

    A. it would enhance traditional memory-based arts of rhetoric

    B. it would make learners more forgetful and rely less on their memories

    C. it would bring truth and knowledge to learners

    D. it would make learners appear wise but, in reality, know nothing

2. Which of the following best summarizes the main purpose of assigning essay writing?

    A. To showcase high grades to parents and create a sense of pride.

    B. To encourage critical thinking, research skills, and effective expression of ideas.

    C. To test students' ability to memorize and recall information.

    D. To highlight the importance of employing artificial intelligence.

3. One of the main benefits of using ChatGPT in education is that it can _____.

    A. generate high-quality essays for students

    B. replace the need for teachers in the classroom

    C. help students research and generate building blocks for essays

    D. create a more punitive environment for students

4. What does the author suggest as a potential downside of using ChatGPT in schools with fewer resources?

    A. Students may not obtain useful skills and end up with plagiarized essays.

    B. Teachers may have to provide more detailed feedback, which could be burdensome.

Extensive Reading 3

C. The use of conversational AI could exacerbate inequalities in education.

D. It could lead to increased trust and better essay quality.

5. According to the text, how does the value of attention change with the overwhelming amount of information available?

   A. The value of attention increases.

   B. The value of attention remains the same.

   C. The value of attention decreases.

   D. The value of attention is not discussed in the text.

6. What does the author propose as the way forward in response to technological advances like AI?

   A. Resisting the process and maintaining traditional methods of gathering information.

   B. Lamenting the loss of supplanted skills and not adapting to new ones.

   C. Relying solely on ChatGPT to guide us in the right direction.

   D. Developing policies that ensure equitable education and better working conditions for all.

Reasoning and Analyzing

Answer the following questions.

1. What limitations does the author identify in using ChatGPT for educational purposes?

   _____

   _____

2. Can you find an expression which delivers meaning similar to "high-quality intellectual snow job" (Para. 8)? What do both phrases suggest?

   _____

   _____

3. According to the author, how can ChatGPT be incorporated into education in a beneficial way?

   _____

   _____

4. How does the author argue that reliance on ChatGPT can lead to inequalities in education?

   _____

   _____

5. "In schools with fewer resources, some students may end up turning in AI-produced essays." (Para. 16) "Some school officials may treat this as a problem of merely plagiarism detection and expand the use of draconian surveillance systems." (Para. 17) What does the author think of the surveillance systems adopted by these schools?

Unit 8 Key Elements of Arguments: Assumptions

6. What does the author imply by "a wealth of information creates a poverty of attention" (Para. 20)?

7. Plato claimed that "the use of text would threaten traditional memory-based arts of rhetoric." (Para. 1) How does the author challenge Plato's view on the role of memory in learning?

8. What does the author imply in her final assessment of ChatGPT's ability to guide society in addressing these challenges?

✈ Reflecting and Creating

Activity 1 Recognize and Evaluate Assumptions

The following are some arguments from the essay. Recognize the hidden assumptions, and then evaluate them.

1. According to the text, Plato argued that the invention of the alphabet would lead to "forgetfulness in the learners' souls because they will not use their memories". (Para. 1) What are the assumptions underlying the argument? Do you share the assumptions?

2. The author claims: "Unless sufficient resources are provided equitably, adapting to conversational AI in flipped classrooms could exacerbate inequalities." What are the hidden assumptions in the argument? Do you accept the assumptions as true and reliable?

3. The article states: "Educational approaches that treat students like enemies may teach students to hate or subvert the controls. That's not a recipe for human betterment." What are the assumptions underlying this argument? Please evaluate the assumptions.

4. According to the author, "If AI enhances the value of education for some while degrading the education of others, the promise of betterment will be broken." What are the assumptions underlying the argument? Do you share the assumptions?

_____

_____

5. As societies responded to previous technological advances, the author argues, regarding ChatGPT or other AI tools, "we will also need policies that allow more people to live with dignity as a basic right, even if their skills have been superseded." (Para. 28) What are the assumptions underlying the argument? What do you think about the assumptions?

_____

_____

Activity 2 Topics for Discussion and Writing

1. The essay discusses the impact of ChatGPT on education. It argues, "It is in high schools and even college where some of ChatGPT's most interesting and troubling aspects will become clear." Have you ever used ChatGPT? If yes, what did you use it for? If not, how much do you know about ChatGPT and its applications in education? What roles do you envision students, teachers, and ChatGPT taking on in the context of education? How can they collaborate effectively? Have a discussion on these questions in small groups.

2. The author argues that ChatGPT can be used as a tool in flipped classrooms, where students "generate critically examined building blocks of essays". Have you ever experienced a flipped classroom setting? If yes, do you think this is an effective approach? If not, do you prefer learning in a flipped classroom? What are the advantages of a flipped classroom over a traditional classroom? What strategies or tools do you think would be effective in supporting a flipped classroom environment? What are the potential concerns or disadvantages of a flipped classroom approach? Write a short essay responding to the above questions.

Unit 8 Key Elements of Arguments: Assumptions

Summary

Self-reflection

Fill out the checklist.

Area	Yes / No?	Notes / Comment
I know what assumptions are.		
I can identify explicit and implicit assumptions.		
I know the audience may not share the author's assumptions.		
I know the differences between factual assumptions, analytical assumptions, and assumptions related to values and beliefs.		
I know how to identify implicit assumptions in arguments.		
I know how to examine different types of assumptions.		

Value Cultivation

Quotes Exploration: Translate the following quotes into English or Chinese and have a discussion about them in small groups.

1. 纸上得来终觉浅，绝知此事要躬行。——董其昌《画旨》
2. 教育数字化是我国开辟教育发展新赛道和塑造教育发展新优势的重要突破口。进一步推进数字教育，为个性化学习、终身学习、扩大优质教育资源覆盖面和教育现代化提供有效支撑。

　　　　　　　　　　——习近平总书记在中共中央政治局第五次集体学习时的讲话

3. The mind is not a vessel to be filled but a fire to be kindled. —Plutarch
4. The real danger is not that computers will begin to think like men, but that men will begin to think like computers. —Sydney J. Harris

Extensive Reading 3

Further Reading

1. 《习近平总书记教育重要论述讲义》（英文版）
2. "On Education" by Albert Einstein
3. "ChatGPT: A Threat to Higher Education?" by Jason Wingard